THE SCIENCE OF GETTING RICH

A Lawful Process for the Creation of Wealth

By

WALLACE D. WATTLES

To Reorder
BLUE RIBBON VIDEO
1-800-533-2885

LifeSuccess Productions

Phoenix, Arizona

LifeSuccess Productions
15651 N. 83rd Way, Suite C3
Scottsdale, AZ 85260
800-871-9715
800-317-9679 Fax

Copyright © 1996 by LifeSuccess Productions

All rights reserved. No part of this book may be
reproduced or utilized in any form or by any means,
electronic or mechanical, including photocopying,
recording, or by any information storage and retrieval
system, without permission in writing from the publisher.

Cover Design: Van Crosby
                    EpiCenter Design

Front Cover Photography: Miron J. Dorf

Printed and bound in the United States of America.

ISBN 0-9656264-0-7

10 9 8 7 6 5 4 3 2 1

Contents

The Little Green Book..*v*

Introduction ....*xi*

1. The Right to be Rich 1

2. There is a Science of Getting Rich 5

3. Is Opportunity Monopolized? 11

4. The First Principle in the Science of Getting Rich....15

5. Increasing Life 23

6. How Riches Come To You 31

7. Gratitude 37

8. Thinking in the Certain Way 43

9. How to Use the Will 49

10. Further Use of the Will 55

11. Acting in the Certain Way 63

12. Efficient Action 71

13. Getting Into the Right Business 77

14. The Impression of Increase 83

15. The Advancing Man 89

16. Some Cautions and Concluding Observations 95

17. A Summary of the Science of Getting Rich 101

    Questions 105

DEDICATED TO MARGIE

The Little Green Book

Lloyd Conant would gently raise his hand in the air and leave it suspended in space. His head would tilt slightly back and the look in his eyes would have you thinking that he was staring right through the roof at some magnificent image high in the sky. With a slight smile on his face, he would speak in a quiet but confident tone and before you knew it, your mind was travelling with his.

Lloyd called what he was doing "imagineering" and whomever was present would be going on a journey of the mind to BE or DO whatever Lloyd chose. It was always a soul-awakening trip with Lloyd Conant at the helm. He sure knew how to take the lid off your mind.

One evening in 1969, Harold Gash from Little Rock, Arkansas and I were guests in Lloyd's home; he was taking us on one of those wild and wonderful trips. We were sitting in his kitchen after dinner. The three of us were busy building castles in space. Reflecting back on that evening many years ago, I realize how much Lloyd was enjoying himself. There he was in his kitchen, inspiring two of his top lieutenants, explaining how we were going to put Earl Nightingale's motivational/educational recordings in every home in the world.

Lloyd Conant believed everyone had infinite potential and we were going to make them aware of this beautiful truth. Harold and I both believed every word Lloyd said and we were ready to do whatever he asked of us. I might add that everyone who ever worked with Lloyd Conant would have nothing but good things to say about him. Lloyd was a beautiful human being who dedicated his life to making the world a better place for everyone. I always felt that Earl Nightingale was fortunate to have Lloyd Conant as a business partner.

It was on that evening in 1969 when Lloyd told Harold and me about "the little green book". That entire evening is so fresh in my mind I can still hear Lloyd's voice. He began to speak very softly and it was obvious that, as he spoke, he was travelling into the past in his mind. He explained how, many years before, he had been given this "little green book". You could feel Lloyd's energy change as he held the image of that little green book in his mind. He told Harold and me that he stayed home all weekend reading and rereading its contents, and how he was absolutely fascinated with the way the author shared such profound wisdom. Then on Monday morning he decided he would build a world-class corporation.

Anyone who knows of the Nightingale-Conant Corporation is aware that Lloyd Conant did exactly what he said after studying the contents of "the little green book". To me, the Nightingale-Conant Corporation today stands as a monument to Lloyd Conant's dream, to his vision, and to his understanding of "the little green book".

Throughout Lloyd's conversation, I was bursting with curiosity to know the title of "the little green book" and even more so, what was written in this magical text. I am sure you must be as well ....

You are holding "the little green book" in your hands. It was Wallace D. Wattles' masterpiece <u>The Science of Getting Rich</u>. Lloyd gave both of us a copy but I later found out that Harold Gash had owned a copy for some time and was already successfully applying Wattles' philosophy.

At the time Lloyd gave me this book I had been a serious student of human potential for close to ten years. I had been studying Earl Nightingale's material since shortly after he began recording his philosophy. I have been fortunate, very fortunate, in having many great mentors/teachers in my life. Lloyd Conant and Earl Nightingale were two of them. The "little green book" however, moved me into an entirely different dimension of thought and ultimately a much deeper understanding of the truth. The contents of this book have served as the foundation for every personal development program I have written for the past quarter century.

Books have the power to change a person's life. This "little green book" had quite a profound affect on Lloyd Conant's life, as it has on mine. Through serious study of its content, this book will most certainly improve the quality of your life.

Wallace D. Wattles directs the reader in the introduction to follow his instruction to the letter, without question. *I was not able to do that.* As I have already mentioned, I had been seriously seeking answers to some very heavy questions for almost ten years prior to Mr. Wattles entering my life. The Science of Getting Rich answered many questions which had been running around my mind. However, it also raised many other powerful questions which required answers. I learned many years ago that every question brings with it, the answer. You cannot have one without the other, any more than you can have an up without a down, or a hot without a cold. There is a law of polarity in the universe which decrees everything has an opposite. Thus question, ... answer.

My years of research, coupled with the rich experience I have gained from my work, has cast a bright light on many of the answers I have been seeking. I have written a number of very powerful seminars and I have taught these seminars worldwide, from Asia to America. My seminars have assisted companies to increase their business by hundreds of millions of dollars each year. The ideas and exercises in these recorded and live seminars have directed many thousands of individuals to lead richer, brighter lives. This valuable information has enabled me to mentor educators, psychiatrists, medical doctors, senior executives from multinational corporations as well as students and salespeople. Without exception, every one of these individuals can see and enjoy a brighter future because of their new awareness.

Realizing the impact information of this nature can have on a person's life, has caused me to be totally committed to teaching these concepts for the rest of my stay on our tiny planet.

A few months ago while I was talking with Gina Robichaud, a very valuable business associate of mine for over ten years, I made a big decision. Gina and I were discussing this book and how it actually represented the foundation of all my seminars. We decided that I would write a foreword to "the little green book" and the two of us would publish it. Then a few days later, I made another decision. Along with the release of the book I would prepare a complete seminar on The Science of Getting Rich. Of all the work I have done in this field over the past twenty-five to thirty years, I believe this to be my most important by far. This book will certainly awaken something in you that will change your life.

If you want to accelerate your progress, make a quick start ... the recorded Science of Getting Rich seminar, complete with the Income Acceleration Guide, is now available.

As you read this book, make up your mind that you will revisit each page frequently until your personal financial goals are realized. Refuse to let your present results influence your thinking. Keep reminding yourself that you have a power within you that is superior to any condition or circumstance you may encounter enroute to your goal.

It is my sincere hope that you find in this "little green book" what I have been enjoying for many wonderful years.

Bob Proctor

Introduction

The book is pragmatical, not philosophical. It is a practical manual, not a treatise on theories. It is intended for the men and women whose most pressing need is for money—for people who wish to get rich first and philosophize afterward. It is for those who have, so far, found neither the time, the means nor the opportunity to go deeply into the study of metaphysics. It is intended for those who want results and who are willing to take the conclusions of science as a basis for action—without going into all the processes by which those conclusions were reached.

I expect the reader to take my statements on faith just as he would take statements concerning a law of electrical action if they were promulgated by a Marconi or an Edison. By taking these statements on faith, he will prove their truth by acting upon them without fear or hesitation. Every man or woman who does this will certainly get rich. The science of this book is an exact science, and failure is impossible.

In writing this book I have used plain style so that all might understand. The following plan of action has been thoroughly tested and bears the supreme test for any practical experiment: it works.

1

The Right to be Rich

Whatever may be said in praise of poverty, the fact remains that it is not possible to live a really complete or successful life unless one is rich. No person can rise to his greatest possible height in talent or soul development unless he has plenty of money. In order to unfold the soul and to develop talent he must have many things to use, and he cannot have these things unless he has money to buy them with. It is important for you to remember that spirit awaits direction from the soul. "Ask and it shall be given," was excellent advice.

People develop in mind, soul, and body by making use of things, and society is so organized that people must have money in order to become the possessor of things. Therefore, the basis of all human advancement must be the science of getting rich.

The object of all life is development. Everything that lives has an inalienable right to all the development it is capable of attaining.

A person's right to life means his right to have the free and unrestricted use of all the things which may be necessary to his fullest mental, spiritual and physical unfolding—in other words, his right to be rich.

In this book, I shall not speak of riches in a figurative way. To be really rich does not mean to be satisfied or contented with a little. No person ought to be satisfied with a little if he is capable of using and enjoying more. The purpose of nature is the advancement and development of life. Every individual should have all that can contribute to the power, elegance, beauty, and richness of life.

The person who owns all he wants for the living of all the life he is capable of living is rich. Nobody can have all he wants without plenty of money. Life has advanced so far and become so complex that even the most ordinary man or woman requires a great amount of wealth in order to live in a manner that even approaches completeness. Every person naturally wants to become all that he is capable of becoming; this desire to realize innate possibilities is inherent in human nature. Success in life is becoming what you want to be. You can become what you want to be only by making use of things, and you can have the free use of things only as you become rich enough to buy them. Therefore, an understanding of the science of getting rich is the most essential of all knowledge.

There is nothing wrong in wanting to get rich. The desire for riches is really the desire for a richer, fuller, and more abundant life. And, that desire is praiseworthy. The person who does not desire to live more abundantly is uncommon. And the individual who does not desire to have money

enough to buy all he wants may not be living to
his full potential.

There are three motives for which we live: we
live for the body, the mind, and the soul. No one
of these is better or holier than the other. Each
is desirable, and neither body, mind, nor soul can
live fully if one of the others is cut short of full
life and expression. It is not right or noble to
live only for the soul and deny mind or body. It
is wrong to live for the intellect and deny body
and soul.

We are all acquainted with the loathsome
consequences of living for the body and denying
both mind and soul. We see that real life means
the complete expression of all that a person can
give forth through body, mind, and soul. No
person can be really happy or satisfied unless his
body is living fully in every function and unless
the same is true of his mind and his soul.
Wherever there is an unexpressed possibility or
an unperformed function, there is an unsatisfied
desire. Desire is possibility seeking expression
or function seeking performance.

A person cannot live fully in body without
good food, comfortable clothing, warm shelter,
and freedom from excessive toil. Rest and
recreation are also necessary to his physical life.

He cannot live fully in mind without books and
time to study them, without opportunity for travel
and observation, or without intellectual
companionship. To live fully in mind he must have
intellectual recreations and must surround

himself with all the objects of art and beauty he is capable of using and appreciating.

To live fully in soul an individual must have love. And the expression of love is often frustrated by poverty.

An individual's highest happiness is found in the bestowal of benefits on those he loves. Love finds its most natural and spontaneous expression in giving. The person who has nothing to give cannot fill his place as a husband or father, as a citizen, or as a human being. It is in the use of material things, that a person finds full life for his body, develops his mind, and unfolds his soul. It is therefore of supreme importance to be rich.

It is perfectly right that you should desire to be rich. If you are a normal man or woman you cannot help doing so. It is perfectly right that you should give your best attention to the science of getting rich because it is the noblest and most necessary of all studies. If you neglect this study, you are derelict in your duty to yourself, to God, and to humanity. You can render God and humanity no greater service than to make the most of yourself.

> "God's gift to you is more talent and ability than you could possibly use in your lifetime. Your gift to God is to develop as much of that talent and ability as you can in this lifetime."
>
> Steve Bow

2

There is a Science of Getting Rich

There is a science of getting rich. It is an exact science, like algebra or arithmetic. There are certain laws which govern the process of acquiring riches. Once a person learns and obeys these laws, he will get rich with mathematical certainty.

There is but one Great Law: namely, "Energy Is."

All physical and mental science is based on this one great law and its seven subsidiary laws which operate in co-ordination with each other:

1. The Law of Perpetual Transmutation
2. The Law of Relativity
3. The Law of Vibration
4. The Law of Polarity
5. The Law of Rhythm
6. The Law of Cause and Effect
7. The Law of Gender.

The best definition of Natural Law seems to be that, "It is the uniform and orderly method of the omnipotent God."

Unlike any other form of animal life that has been created, we were given the power of choice or free will; along with this power came certain responsibilities. The capacity to choose does not involve freedom from the consequence of our choice. The laws or rules which govern every man and which we cover to some degree in this book, are as exact as the laws which govern the material universe. You can act in accordance with these laws or you can disregard them, but you cannot in any way alter them. The law forever operates and holds you to strict accountability, and there is not the slightest allowance made for ignorance.

The ownership of money and property comes as a result of doing things in a certain way. Those who do things in this certain way, whether on purpose or accidentally, get rich. Those who do not do things in this certain way, no matter how hard they work or how able they are, remain poor.

It is a natural law that like causes always produce like effects. Therefore, any man or woman who learns to do things in this certain way will infallibly get rich.

That the above statement is true is shown by the following facts.

Getting rich is not a matter of environment. If it were, all the people in certain areas would become wealthy. The people of one city would all be rich, while those of other towns would all be poor. The inhabitants of one state would roll in wealth, while those of an adjoining state would be in poverty.

We frequently see rich and poor living in the same environment and often engaged in the same vocations. When two people are in the same locality and in the same business—and one gets rich while the other remains poor—it shows that getting rich is not primarily a matter of environment. Some environments may be more favorable than others, but when two people in the same business are in the same neighborhood—and one gets rich while the other fails—it indicates that getting rich is the result of doing things in a certain way.

And, furthermore, the ability to do things in this certain way is not due solely to the possession of talent, because many people who have great talent remain poor, while others who have very little talent get rich.

If we study people who have gotten rich, we find that they are an average lot in all respects. It is evident that they do not get rich because they possess unique talents and abilities. They get rich because they happen to do things in a certain way.

Getting rich is not the result of saving or thrift. Many very penurious people are poor, while free spenders often get rich.

Nor is getting rich due to doing things which others fail to do. Two people in the same business often do almost exactly the same things, and one gets rich while the other remains poor or becomes bankrupt.

From all these things, we must come to the conclusion that getting rich is the result of doing things in a certain way.

If getting rich is the result of doing things in a certain way, then any man or woman who can do things in that way can become rich. And if like causes always produce like effects, the whole matter can be brought within the domain of an exact science.

The question arises whether this certain way may not be so difficult that only a few may follow it. As we have seen, this cannot be true so far as natural ability is concerned. Talented people get rich, and blockheads get rich. Intellectually brilliant people get rich, and very stupid people get rich. Physically strong people get rich, and weak and sickly people get rich.

Some degree of ability to think and understand is, of course, essential. But, in so far as natural ability is concerned, any man or woman who has sense enough to read and understand these words can certainly get rich.

Although we have seen that it is not a matter of environment, location does count for something. One would not go to the heart of the Sahara and expect to do successful business.

Getting rich involves the necessity of dealing with people and of being where there are people to deal with. But, that is about as far as environment matters. If anybody else in your town can get rich, so can you. If anybody else in your state can get rich, so can you.

Again, it is not a matter of choosing some particular business or profession. People get rich in every business and in every profession— while their next door neighbors in the same vocation remain in poverty.

It is true that you will do best in a business which you like. And, if you have certain talents which are well developed, you will do best in a business which calls for the exercise of those talents.

Also, you will do best in a business which is suited to your locality. An ice cream parlor would do better in a warm climate than in Greenland. A salmon fishery will succeed better in the Northwest than in Florida where there are no salmon.

But, aside from these general limitations, getting rich is not dependent on your engaging in some particular business, but on your learning to do things in a certain way. If you are now in business—and someone else in your locality is getting rich in the same business, while you are not getting rich—it is because you are not doing things in the same way that the other person is doing them.

No one is prevented from getting rich by lack of capital. True, as you get capital, its increase becomes more easy and rapid. But, no matter how poor you may be—if you begin to do things in a certain way—you will begin to have capital. The getting of capital is a part of the process of getting rich. It is a part of the result which invariably follows the doing of things in a certain way.

You may be the poorest person on the continent and be deeply in debt, but if you begin to do things in this certain way, you must infallibly begin to get rich. Because like causes must produce like effects, you will get rich even if you do not have any friends, influence, or other resources. If you have no capital, you can get capital. If you are in the wrong business, you can get into the right business. If you are in the wrong location, you can go to the right location. You can do so by beginning in your present business and in your present location to do things in a certain way which causes success. You must begin to live in harmony with the laws that govern the universe.

3

Is Opportunity Monopolized?

No person is kept poor because opportunity has been taken away from him—because other people have monopolized the wealth and have put a fence around it. You may decide not to engage in certain kinds of business, but there are other channels open to you.

At different periods the tide of opportunity moves in different directions, according to the needs of the whole and to the particular stage of social evolution which has been reached.

There is an abundance of opportunity for the man or woman who will go with the tide, instead of trying to swim against it.

Office workers, either as individuals or as a group, are not deprived of opportunity. The workers are not being kept down by their masters—by the powers of big business and the conglomerates. As a group, they are where they are because they do things in a certain way.

When it begins to do things in a certain way, the working class can become the master class. The law of wealth is the same for it as it is for all other groups. Workers will remain where they are as long as they continue to do as they do. The individual worker, however, is not held down by the ignorance or the mental slothfulness of his class; he can follow the tide of opportunity to riches. This book will tell him how.

No one is kept in poverty by a shortness in the supply of riches. There is more than enough for all. A palace as large as the capitol at Washington could be built for every family on earth from the building material available in the United States alone. Under intensive cultivation, this country could produce enough wool, cotton, linen, silk, and food to clothe and feed each person in the world. The visible supply is practically inexhaustible. And, the invisible supply really is inexhaustible.

Everything you see on earth is made from one original substance, out of which all things proceed. New forms are constantly being made and older ones are dissolving, but all are shapes assumed by one thing.

There is no limit to the supply of formless stuff or original substance. The universe is made out of it, but it was not all used in making the universe. The spaces in, through, and between the forms of the visible universe are permeated and filled with the original substance—with the formless stuff, with the raw material of all things. Ten thousand universes can still be made, and even then, the supply of universal raw material will not be exhausted.

No person, therefore, is poor because nature is poor or because there is not enough to go around.

Nature is an inexhaustible storehouse of riches. The supply will never run short. Original substance is alive with creative energy and is constantly producing more forms. When the supply of building material is exhausted, more will be produced. When the soil is exhausted so that foodstuffs and materials for clothing will no longer grow upon it, it will be renewed or more soil will be made. When all the gold and silver has been dug from the earth—if human beings are still in such a stage of social development as to need gold and silver—more will be produced from the formless. The formless stuff responds to the needs of humans; it will not let them be without any good thing.

This is true of man collectively. The race as a whole is always abundantly rich. If individuals are poor, it is because they do not follow a certain way of doing things which makes the individual man rich.

The formless stuff is intelligent; it is material which thinks. It is alive and is always impelled toward more life.

It is the natural and inherent impulse of life to seek to live more. It is the nature of intelligence to enlarge itself and the quality of consciousness to seek to extend its boundaries and find fuller expression. The universe of forms has been made by formless living substance, throwing itself into form in order to express itself more fully.

The universe is a great living presence, always

moving inherently toward more life and fuller functioning.

Nature is formed for the advancement of life; its motive is the increase of life. For this reason, everything which can possibly minister to life is bountifully provided. There can be no lack unless God is to contradict himself and nullify his own works.

You are not kept poor by a shortness in the supply of riches. I shall demonstrate a little farther on that even the resources of the formless supply are at the command of any man or woman who will act and think in a certain way.

4

The First Principle in the Science of Getting Rich

Thought is the only power which can produce tangible riches from the formless substance. The stuff from which all things are made is a substance which thinks. A thought of form in this substance produces the form.

Original substance moves according to its thoughts. Every form and process you see in nature is the visible expression of a thought in the original substance. As it thinks of a form, it takes that form; as it thinks of a motion, it makes that motion. That is the way all things were created. We live in a thought world, and this world is a part of a thought universe.

The thought of a moving universe extended throughout the formless substance. The thinking stuff resulting from that thought, took the form of systems of planets and continues to maintain that form. Thinking substance takes the form of its thought and moves according to the thought. Holding the idea of a circling system of suns and worlds, it took the form of these bodies, and moved them accordingly.

Although centuries may be required to do the work, by thinking the form of a slow growing tree, the formless substance produces the tree. In creating, the formless substance seems to move according to the lines of motion it has established. The thought of an oak tree does not cause the instant formation of a full grown tree, but it does start in motion the forces which will produce the tree along established lines of growth.

Every thought of form, held in thinking substance, causes the creation of that form—but always, or at least generally, along lines of growth and action already established.

If the thought of a house of a certain construction were impressed upon the formless substance, it might not cause the instant formation of that house. But, it would cause the turning of creative energies already working in trade and commerce into such channels as to result in the speedy building of the house. And, if there were no existing channels through which the creative energy could work, the house would be formed directly from primal substance—without waiting for the slow processes of the organic and inorganic world.

No thought of form can be impressed upon the original substance without causing the creation of that form.

A human being is a thinking center and can originate thought. All the forms that a person fashions with his hands must first emerge from his thought. He cannot shape a thing until he has thought that thing.

And, so far man has confined his efforts wholly to the work of his hands; he has applied manual labor to the world of forms—seeking to change or modify already existing forms. He has never thought of trying to cause the creation of new forms by impressing his thoughts upon the formless substance.

When a person has a thought form, he takes material from the forms of nature and makes an image of the form which is in his mind. He has, so far, made little or no effort to cooperate with the formless intelligence—to work 'with the Father.' He has not dreamed that he can do what he seeth the Father doing. Man reshapes and modifies existing forms by manual labor. He has not considered the question of whether he could produce things from the formless substance by communicating his thoughts to it. I propose to prove that he may do so, to prove that any man or woman may do so, and to show how. My first step will be to lay down three fundamental propositions.

First, we assert that there is one original formless substance from which all things are made. All the seemingly many elements are only different presentations of one element. All the many forms found in organic and inorganic nature are only different shapes made from the same stuff. And, this stuff is thinking stuff; a thought held in it produces the form of the thought. Thought, in thinking substance, produces shapes. A human being is a thinking center, capable of original thought. If a person can communicate his thought to original thinking substance, he can cause the creation or formation of the thing he thinks about. To summarize this:

There is a thinking stuff from which all things are made, and which, in its original state, permeates, penetrates, and fills the interspaces of the universe.

A thought in this substance produces the thing that is imaged by the thought.

A person can form things in his thought, and by impressing his thought upon formless substance, can cause the thing he thinks about to be created.

I can prove these statements by both logic and experience. Reasoning back from the phenomena of form and thought, I come to one original thinking substance. And, reasoning forward from this thinking substance, I come to the individual's power to cause the formation of the thing he thinks about.

By experiment, I find this reasoning to be true, and this is my strongest proof. If one person who reads this book gets rich by doing what I tell him to do, that is evidence in support of my claim. Furthermore, if every person who does what I tell him to do gets rich, that is positive proof until someone goes through the process and fails. The theory is true until the process fails, and this process will not fail because every person who does exactly what I tell him to do will get rich.

I have said that an individual gets rich by doing things in a certain way. In order to do so, a person must become able to think in a certain way. A person's way of doing things is the direct result of the way he thinks about things.

To do things in a way you want to do them, you will have to acquire the ability to think the way you want to think. This is the first step toward getting rich. To think what you want to think is to think *truth* regardless of appearances.

Every person has the natural and inherent power to think what he wants to think, but it requires far more effort to do so than it does to think the thoughts which are suggested by appearances. To think according to appearances is easy. To think truth regardless of appearances is laborious and requires the expenditure of more power than any other work a person has to perform.

There is no labor from which most people shrink as they do from that of sustained and consecutive thought; it is the hardest work in the world. This is especially true when truth is contrary to appearances. Every appearance in the visible world tends to produce a corresponding form in the mind which observes it. This can only be prevented by holding the thought of the *truth*.

To look upon the appearance of disease will produce the form of disease in your own mind— and ultimately in your body. Instead you must hold the thought of the *truth,* which is that there is no disease. Disease is only an appearance, and the reality is health.

To look upon the appearances of poverty will produce corresponding forms in your own mind. Instead, you must hold to the truth that there is no poverty. There is only abundance.

It requires power to think health when surrounded by the appearances of disease, or to think riches when in the midst of the appearances of poverty. But, he who acquires this power becomes a master mind. He can conquer fate; he can have what he wants.

This power can only be acquired by getting hold of the basic fact which is behind all appearances: that there is one thinking substance, from which and by which all things are made.

Then, we must grasp the truth that every thought held in this substance becomes a form and that a person can impress his thoughts upon it so as to cause them to take form and become visible things.

When we realize this, we lose all doubt and fear because we know that we can create what we want to create. We can get what we want to have and can become what we want to be. As a first step toward getting rich, you must believe the three fundamental statements given previously in this chapter. In order to emphasize them, I will repeat them here:

There is a thinking stuff from which all things are made, and which, in its original state, permeates, penetrates, and fills the interspaces of the universe.

A thought in this substance produces the thing that is imaged by the thought.

A person can form things in his thought, and by impressing his thought upon formless substance, can cause the thing he thinks about to be created.

You must lay aside all other concepts of the universe than this monistic one. You must dwell upon this until it is fixed in your mind and has become your habitual thought. Read these creed statements over and over again. Fix every word upon your memory, and meditate upon them until you firmly believe what they say. If a doubt comes to you, cast it aside as a sin. Do not listen to arguments against this idea; do not go to churches or lectures where a contrary concept of things is taught or preached. Do not read magazines or books which teach a different idea. If you get mixed up in your faith, all your efforts will be in vain.

Do not ask why these things are true, nor speculate as to how they can be true. Simply take them on trust.

The science of getting rich begins with the absolute acceptance of this faith.

5

Increasing Life

Y ou must get rid of the last vestige of the old idea that there is a deity whose will it is that you should be poor or whose purposes may be served by keeping you in poverty. God loves you and wants you to live an abundant life.

The intelligent substance, which is everything and lives in everything, lives in you. It is a consciously living substance. Being a consciously living substance, it must have the natural and inherent desire of every living intelligence for the increase of life. Every living thing must continually seek for the enlargement of its life because life—in the mere act of living—must increase itself.

A seed, dropped into the ground, springs into activity, and in the act of living, produces a hundred more seeds. Life, by living, multiplies itself. It is forever becoming more; it must do so to continue to exist.

Intelligence is under this same necessity for continuous increase. Every thought we think makes it necessary for us to think another thought. Consciousness is continually expanding. Every fact we learn leads us to the learning of another fact. Knowledge is continually increasing. Every talent we cultivate brings to the mind the desire to cultivate another talent. We are subject to the urge of life. In seeking expression for this urge, we are impelled to know more, to do more, and to be more.

In order to know more, do more, and be more, we must have more. We must have things to use because we learn and do and become only by using things. We must get rich so that we can live more.

The desire for riches is simply the capacity for larger life seeking fulfillment; every desire is the effort of an unexpressed possibility to come into action. It is power seeking to manifest which causes desire. That which makes you want more money is the same as that which makes the plant grow. It is life, seeking fuller expression.

The one living substance must be subject to this law for all of life. It is permeated with the desire to live more; that is why it is under the necessity of creating things. Because this substance desires to live more in you, it wants you to have all the things you can use.

It is the desire of God that you should get rich. He wants you to get rich because he can express himself better through you if you have plenty of things to use in giving him expression. He can live more in you if you have unlimited command of the means of life.

The universe desires you to have everything you want to have. Nature is friendly to your plans. Everything is naturally for you. Make up your mind that this is true.

It is essential, however, that your purpose

should harmonize with the purpose that is in everything.

You must want real life, not mere pleasure or sensual gratification. Life is the performance of function, and the individual really lives only when he performs without excess every function— physical, mental, and spiritual—of which he is capable.

You do not want to get rich in order to live swinishly for the gratification of animal desires. That is not life. But, the performance of every physical function is a part of life, and no one lives completely who denies the impulses of the body a normal and healthful expression.

You do not want to get rich solely to enjoy mental pleasures, to get knowledge, to gratify ambition, to outshine others, or to be famous. All these are a legitimate part of life; however, the person who only lives for the pleasures of the intellect alone will only have a partial life. He will never be satisfied with his lot.

You do not want to get rich solely for the good of others. Nor do you wish to lose yourself for the salvation of humanity or to only experience the joys of philanthropy and sacrifice. The joys of the soul are only a part of life. They are no better or nobler than any other part.

You want to get rich so that you can eat, drink, and be merry when it is time to do these things. You want to be rich so that you may surround yourself with beautiful things, see distant lands, feed your mind, and develop your intellect. You want to be rich so that you may love people, do kind things, and be able to play a good part in helping the world to find truth.

But, remember that extreme altruism is no better and no nobler than extreme selfishness. Both are mistakes.

Get rid of the idea that God wants you to sacrifice yourself for others, that you can secure his favor by doing so. God requires nothing of the kind.

What he wants is that you should make the most of yourself—for yourself, and for others. And, you can help others more by making the most of yourself than in any other way.

You can make the most of yourself only by getting rich. Thus, it is right and praiseworthy that you should give your first and best thought to the work of acquiring wealth.

Remember, however, that the desire of substance is for all. Its movements must be for more life to all; it cannot be made to work for less life to any because it is seeking riches and life in everything and in everyone.

The intelligent substance will make things for you, but it will not take things away from someone else and give them to you.

You must get rid of the thought of competition. You are to create, not to compete for what is already created. You do not have to take anything away from anyone. You do not have to drive sharp bargains. You do not have to cheat or to take advantage. You do not need to let any person work for you for less than he earns.

You do not have to covet the property of others or to look at it with wishful eyes. No one has anything of which you cannot have the same. And, you can have it without taking what he has away from him.

You are to become a creator, not a competitor. You will become a creator by employing the higher faculties with which you have been endowed: ***Perception, Reason, Will, Memory, Imagination*** and ***Intuition***. No other form of life was given these creative faculties. You are going to get what you want, but in such a way that when you get it every other person will have more than he has now.

I am aware that there are people who acquire a vast amount of money by proceeding in direct opposition to the directions in the preceding paragraph. Those of the plutocratic type, who become very rich, sometimes do so purely through their extraordinary ability on the plane of competition. However, sometimes—for example, in their contribution to the growth of industry—they unconsciously harmonize with substance in its movement toward the betterment of humanity. Rockefeller, Carnegie, Morgan, et al., have been the unconscious agents of the Supreme Power in the necessary work of systematizing and organizing productive industry. Their work has contributed immensely toward increased life for all. They helped to organize production and were soon succeeded by the agents of the multitude, who organized the machinery of distribution.

The multimillionaires are like the monster reptiles of prehistoric eras. They play a necessary part in the evolutionary process, but the same power which produced them will dispose of them. And, it is well to bear in mind that they have never been really rich. A record of the private lives of most of this class will show that they have really been the most abject and wretched of the poor.

Riches secured on the competitive plane are never satisfactory and permanent. They are yours today and another's tomorrow. Remember, if you are to become rich in a scientific and certain way, you must rise entirely out of competitive thought. You must never think for a moment that the supply is limited. You drop into the competitive mind the moment you begin to think that all the money is being 'cornered' and controlled by bankers and others and that you must exert yourself to get laws passed to stop this process. Your power to cause creation will temporarily disappear, and what is worse, you will probably arrest the creative movements you have already instituted.

Know that there are countless millions of dollars' worth of undiscovered gold in the mountains of the earth. Know that if there were not, more would be created from the thinking substance to supply your needs. Know that the money you need will come—even if it is necessary for a thousand people to be led to the discovery of new gold mines tomorrow.

Never look at the visible supply; always look at the limitless riches in the formless substance and know that they are coming to you as fast as you can receive and use them. Nobody, by cornering the visible supply, can prevent you from getting what is yours.

Never allow yourself to think for an instant that all the best building spots will be taken before you get ready to build your house. Never worry about the trusts and combines and get anxious for fear they will soon come to own the whole earth. Never get afraid that you will lose what you want because some other person "beats you to it." That cannot possibly happen. You are not seeking any thing that is possessed by anybody else; you are causing what you want to be created from the formless substance. And, the supply is limitless.

Live By This Absolute Truth

There is a thinking stuff from which all things are made, and which, in its original state, permeates, penetrates, and fills the interspaces of the universe.

A thought in this substance produces the thing that is imaged by the thought.

A person can form things in his thought, and by impressing his thought upon formless substance, can cause the thing he thinks about to be created.

6

How Riches Come to You

When I say that you do not have to drive sharp bargains, I do not mean that you do not have to drive any bargains at all or that you are above the necessity for having any dealings with other people. I mean that you will not need to deal with them unfairly; you do not have to get something for nothing. You can give to every person more than you take from them.

You cannot give a person more in cash value than you take from them, but you can give them more in use value than the cash value of the thing you take from them. The paper, ink, and other material in this book may not be worth the money you paid for it. But, if the ideas in this book bring you thousands of dollars, you have not been wronged by those who sold it to you. They have given you a great use value for a small cash value.

Let us suppose that I own a picture which in any civilized community is worth thousands of dollars. I take it to Baffin Bay, and by 'salesmanship' induce an Eskimo to give a bundle of furs worth $500 for it. I have really wronged him because he has no use for the picture. It has no use value to him, it will not add to his life.

But, suppose I give him a gun worth $50 for his furs. Then he has made a good bargain. He has use for the gun; it will get him more furs and much food; it will add to his life in every way; it will make him rich.

When you rise from the competitive to the creative plane, you can scan your business transactions very strictly. If you see that you are selling a person anything which does not add more to his life than the thing he gives you in exchange, you can afford to stop it. You do not have to beat anybody in business. And, if you are in a business which does beat people, get out of it at once.

Give every person more in use value than you take from them in cash value. Then, you are adding to the life of the world with every business transaction.

If you have people working for you, you must take from them more in cash value than you pay them in wages. But, you can organize your business so that it will be filled with the principle of advancement. Thus, each employee who wishes to do so may advance a little every day.

You can make your business do for your employees what this book is doing for you. You can conduct your business so that it will be a ladder by which every willing employee may climb to riches himself. And, it is not your fault if they do not accept the opportunity.

Even though you can cause your riches to come out of the formless substance which permeates all of your environment, it does not follow that your fortune will immediately take shape from the atmosphere and come into being before your eyes.

If you want a sewing machine, for instance, I

would suggest that before you impress the thought of a sewing machine on the thinking substance, you first make sure the image of the machine is clearly formed in your mind. If you want a sewing machine, hold the mental image of it with the most positive certainty that it is being made or is on its way to you. After once forming the thought, have the most absolute and unquestioning faith that the sewing machine is coming. Never think of it or speak of it without feeling confident that it will arrive. Claim it as already yours.

It will be brought to you by the power of the supreme intelligence, acting upon the minds of men. If you live in Maine, it may be that a person will be brought from Texas or Japan to engage in some transaction which will result in your getting what you want. If so, the whole matter will be as much to that person's advantage as it is to yours.

Do not forget for a moment that the thinking substance is in everything, communicating with everything, and able to influence everything. The desire of the thinking substance for more life and better living has caused the creation of all the sewing machines that have ever been made, and it can cause the creation of millions more. It will do so whenever people set it in motion by desire and faith and by acting in the certain way.

You can certainly have a sewing machine in your house. You can have anything you want, as long as you use it for the advancement of your own life and the lives of others.

You need not hesitate about asking largely. "It

is your Father's pleasure to give you the kingdom," said Jesus.

The original substance wants to live as much as possible in you, it wants you to have all that you can or will use for the living of the most abundant life.

Your faith becomes invincible if you fix upon your consciousness the fact that the desire you feel for the possession of riches is one with the desire of the Supreme Power for more complete expression.

Once I saw a little boy sitting at a piano and vainly trying to bring harmony out of the keys. I saw that he was grieved and provoked by his inability to play real music. I asked him why he was unhappy, and he answered, "I can feel the music in me, but I can't make my hands go right." The music in him was the urge of the Original Substance, containing all the possibilities of all life. All that there is of music was seeking expression through the child.

God, the One Substance, is trying to live and do and enjoy things through humanity. He is saying, "I want hands to build wonderful structures, to play divine harmonies, to paint glorious pictures. I want feet to run my errands, eyes to see my beauties, tongues to tell mighty truths and to sing marvelous songs."

All that is possible is seeking expression through human beings. God wants those who can play music to have the instruments they need— to have the means to cultivate their talents to the fullest extent. He wants those who can appreciate beauty to be able to surround themselves with beautiful things. He wants those who can discern truth to have every opportunity to travel and observe. He wants those who can appreciate dress to be beautifully clothed and those who can appreciate good food to be luxuriously fed.

He wants all these things because he enjoys and appreciates them. It is God who wants to play and sing and enjoy beauty and proclaim truth and wear fine clothes and eat good foods.

"It is God that worketh in you to will and to do," said Paul.

The desire you feel for riches is the Infinite, seeking to express himself in you as he sought to find expression in the little boy at the piano.

You need not hesitate to ask largely. Your part is to focus and express the desires of God.

This is a difficult point with most people. They retain something of the old idea that poverty and self-sacrifice are pleasing to God. They look upon poverty as a part of the plan, as a necessity of nature. They have the idea that God has finished his work and has made all that he can make—that the majority of humanity must stay poor because there is not enough to go around. People hold to this erroneous thought so much that they feel ashamed to ask for wealth. They try not to want more than a very modest competence—just enough to make them fairly comfortable.

I recall now the case of one student who was

told that he must see in his mind a clear picture of the things he desired so that the creative thought of them might be impressed on the formless substance. He was a very poor man, living in a rented house and having only what he earned from day to day. He could not grasp the fact that all wealth was his. Therefore, after thinking the matter over, he decided that he might reasonably ask for a new rug for the floor of his best room and an anthracite coal stove to heat the house during the cold weather. Following the instructions given in this book, he obtained these things in a few months. Then it dawned upon him that he had not asked enough. He went through the house in which he lived and planned all the improvements he would like to make in it. He mentally added a bay window here and a room there. He continued until it was complete in his mind as his ideal home. And, then he planned its furnishings.

Holding the whole picture in his mind, he began living in the certain way and moving toward what he wanted. He owns the house now, and is rebuilding it according to his mental image. Now, with still larger faith, he is proceeding to get greater things. It has been unto him according to his faith, and it is so with you and with all of us.

7

Gratitude

The illustrations given in the last chapter will have conveyed to the reader the fact that the first step toward getting rich is to convey the idea of your wants to the formless substance.

This is true, and you will see that in order to do so it becomes necessary to relate yourself to the formless intelligence in a harmonious way.

To secure this harmonious relationship is a matter of such primary and vital importance that I will give some space to its discussion here. I will give you instructions which, if you follow them, will be certain to bring you into a perfect unity of mind with God.

The whole process of mental adjustment and atunement can be summed up in one word: gratitude.

First, you believe that there is one intelligent substance from which all things proceed. Secondly, you believe that this substance gives you everything you desire. And, thirdly, you relate yourself to it through a feeling of deep and profound gratitude.

Many people who order their lives rightly in all other ways are kept in poverty by their lack of gratitude. Having received one gift from God, they cut the wires which connect them with him by failing to make acknowledgment.

It is easy to understand that the nearer we live to the source of wealth, the more wealth we shall receive. It is also easy to understand that a soul that is always grateful lives in closer touch with God than one who never looks to him in thankful acknowledgment.

When good things come to us, the more gratefully we fix our minds on the Supreme Power, the more good things we will receive— and the more rapidly they will come. The reason for this is simply that the mental attitude of gratitude draws the mind into closer touch with the source from which the blessings come.

If it is a new thought to you that gratitude brings your whole mind into closer harmony with the creative energies of the universe, consider it well, and you will see that it is true. The good things you already possess have come to you because of certain laws. Gratitude will lead your mind out along the ways by which things come. And, it will keep you in close harmony with creative thought and prevent you from falling into competitive thought.

Gratitude alone can keep you looking toward the Infinite and prevent you from falling into the error of thinking that the supply of riches is limited—and to think that would be fatal to your hopes.

There is a law of gratitude, and if you are to get the results you seek, it is absolutely necessary that you should observe this law.

The law of gratitude is the natural principle

that action and reaction are always equal and in opposite directions. The grateful outreaching of your mind in thankful praise to the Supreme Power is a liberation or expenditure of force; it cannot fail to reach that to which it is addressed. And, as a result, God responds with an instantaneous movement toward you.

"Draw nigh unto God, and He will draw nigh unto you." That is a statement of psychological truth.

And, if your gratitude is strong and constant, the reaction in the formless substance will be strong and continuous. The movement of the things you want will always be toward you. Notice the grateful attitude that Jesus took—how he always seems to be saying, "I thank Thee, Father, that Thou hearest me." You cannot exercise much power without gratitude, because it is gratitude that keeps you connected with power.

But, the value of gratitude does not consist solely in getting more blessings in the future. Without gratitude you cannot keep from being dissatisfied with things as they are.

The moment you permit your mind to dwell with dissatisfaction upon things as they are, you begin to lose ground. You fix attention upon the common, the poor, the squalid, and the mean— and your mind takes the form of these things. You will then transmit these forms or mental images to the formless. Thus, the common, the poor, the squalid, and the mean will come to you.

To permit your mind to dwell upon the inferior is to become inferior and to surround yourself with inferior things. On the other hand, to fix your attention on the best is to surround yourself with the best and to become the best.

The creative power within us makes us into the image of that to which we give our attention. We are thinking substance, and thinking substance always takes the form of that which it thinks about.

The grateful mind is constantly fixed upon the best. Therefore, it tends to become the best; it takes the form or character of the best and will receive the best.

Also, faith is born of gratitude. The grateful mind continually expects good things, and expectation becomes faith. The reaction of gratitude upon one's own mind produces faith. Every outgoing wave of grateful thanksgiving increases faith. The person who has no feeling of gratitude cannot long retain a living faith. And, as we will see in the following chapters, without a living faith you cannot get rich by the creative method.

It is necessary, then, to cultivate the habit of being grateful for every good thing that comes to you—to give thanks continuously. And, because all things have contributed to your advancement, you should include all things in your gratitude.

Do not waste time thinking or talking about the shortcomings or wrong actions of plutocrats or trust magnates. Their organization of the world has made your opportunity. All that you have received really has come to you because of them.

Do not rage against corrupt politicians. If it were not for politicians we should fall into anarchy, and your opportunity would be greatly lessened.

God has worked a long time and very patiently to bring us up to where we are in industry and government. And he is going right on with his work. I believe that he will do away with plutocrats, trust magnates, captains of industry, and politicians as soon as they can be spared. But, in the meantime, they are very necessary. Remember that they are helping to arrange the lines of transmission along which your riches will come to you. Be grateful to them. This will bring you into a harmonious relationship with the good in everything and the good in everything will move toward you.

8

Thinking in the Certain Way

Turn back to chapter 6. Read again the story of the man who formed a mental image of his house, and you will get a fair idea of the initial step toward getting rich. You must form a clear and definite mental picture of what you want. You cannot transmit an idea unless you have it yourself.

You must have it before you can give it. And, many people fail to impress the thinking substance because they have themselves only a vague and misty concept of the things they want to do, to have, or to become.

It is not enough that you should have a general desire for wealth 'to do good with.' Everybody has that desire.

It is not enough that you should have a wish to travel, see things, live more, etc. Everybody has those desires also. If you were going to send a telegram message to a friend, you would not send the letters of the alphabet in their order and let him construct the message for himself. Nor would you take words at random from the dictionary. You would send a coherent sentence; one which meant something. When you try to impress your wishes upon the thinking substance, remember that it must be done by a coherent statement. You must know what you want, and be definite.

You can never get rich or start the creative power into action by sending out unformed longings and vague desires.

Go over your desires just as the man I have described went over his house. See just what you want and get a clear mental picture of it as you wish it to look when you get it.

As the sailor has the port toward which he is sailing in his mind, you must have a clear mental picture continually in your mind. You must keep your face toward it all the time. You must no more lose sight of it than the steerman loses sight of the compass.

It is not necessary to take exercises in concentration, nor to set apart special times for prayer and affirmation, nor to "go into the silence," nor to do occult stunts of any kind. These things are well enough, but all you need is to know what you want and to want it badly enough so that it will stay in your thoughts.

Spend as much of your leisure time as you can in contemplating your picture. Remember that no one needs to take exercises to concentrate his mind on a thing which he really wants. It is the things you do not really care about which require effort to fix your attention upon them.

Unless your desire to get rich is strong enough to hold your thoughts to the purpose—as the magnetic pole holds the needle of the compass—it will hardly be worth while for you to try to carry out the instructions given in this book.

The methods I am presenting here are for

people whose desire for riches is strong enough to overcome mental laziness and the love of ease.

The more clear and definite you make your picture, and the more you dwell upon it, the stronger your desire will be. And, the stronger your desire, the easier it will be to hold your mind fixed upon the picture of what you want.

However, something more is necessary than merely seeing the picture clearly. If that is all you do, you are only a dreamer and will have little or no power for accomplishment. Behind your clear vision must be the purpose to realize it, to bring it out in tangible expression. And, behind this purpose must be an invincible and unwavering faith that the thing is already yours—that it is at hand and you have only to take possession of it.

Live in the new house mentally until it takes form around you physically. In the mental realm, enter at once into full enjoyment of the things you want.

"Whatsoever things ye ask for when ye pray, believe that ye receive them, and ye shall have them," said Jesus.

See the things you want as if they were actually around you all the time; see yourself as owning and using them. Make use of them in imagination just as you will use them when they are your tangible possessions. Dwell upon your mental picture until it is clear and distinct. Then, take the mental attitude of ownership toward everything in that picture. Take possession of it in your mind in the full faith that it is actually yours. Hold to this mental ownership; do not waver for an instant in the faith that it is real.

And, remember what was said in chapter 7 about gratitude: be as thankful for it all the time as you expect to be when it has taken form. The person who can sincerely thank God for the things which he owns only in imagination has real faith. That person will get rich; that person will cause the creation of whatsoever he wants.

You do not need to pray repeatedly for the things you want. It is not necessary to tell God about it every day. "Use not vain repetitions as the heathen do," said Jesus to his pupils, "for your Father knoweth that ye have need of these things before ye ask Him."

Your part is to intelligently formulate your desire for the things which make for a larger life and to get these desires arranged into a coherent whole. You must then impress this whole desire upon the formless substance, which has the power and the will to bring you what you want.

You do not make this impression by repeating strings of words: you make it by holding the vision with unshakable purpose to attain it—and with steadfast faith that you will attain it.

The answer to prayer is not according to your faith while you are talking, but according to your faith while you are working.

You cannot impress the mind of God by having a special sabbath day set apart to tell him what you want—and then forgetting him during the rest of the week. If you do not think of your prayer until the hour of prayer comes again, you cannot impress him by having special hours to go into your closet and pray.

Oral prayer has its effect in clarifying your vision and strengthening your faith, but it is not your oral petitions which will get you what you want. In order to get rich you do not need a "sweet hour of prayer." You need to "pray without ceasing." And, by prayer, I mean holding steadily to your vision—with the purpose of causing its creation into solid form and the faith that you are doing so.

"Believe that ye receive them."

Once you have clearly formed your vision, the whole matter turns on receiving. When you have formed it, it is well to make an oral statement by addressing the Supreme Power in reverent prayer. From that moment on you must receive in your mind what you ask for. Live in the new house; wear the fine clothes; ride in the automobile; go on the journey, and confidently plan for greater journeys. Think and speak of all the things you have asked for in terms of actual present ownership. Imagine the exact environment and financial condition you desire and live all the time in that imaginary environment and financial condition. Mind, however, that you do not do this as a mere dreamer and castle builder. Hold to the faith that the imaginary is being realized and to the purpose required to realize it. Remember that it is faith and purpose in the use of the imagination which make the difference between the scientist and the dreamer. And, having learned this fact, it is here that you must learn the proper use of the will.

9

How to Use the Will

To set about getting rich in a scientific way, you do not try to apply your will power to anything outside of yourself.

You have no right to do so anyway. It is wrong to apply your will to other men and women in order to get them to do what you wish done.

It is as flagrantly wrong to coerce people by mental power as it is to coerce them by physical power. If compelling people by physical force to do things for you reduces them to slavery, compelling them by mental means accomplishes exactly the same thing. The only difference is in the methods. If taking things from people by physical force is robbery, then taking things by mental force is also robbery. In principle there is no difference.

You have no right to use your will power upon another person—even "for his own good"—because you do not know what is for his good.

The science of getting rich does not require you to apply power or force to any other person, in any way whatsoever. There is not the slightest necessity for doing so. Indeed, any attempt to use your will upon others will only tend to defeat your purpose.

You do not need to apply your will to things for them to come to you. That would simply be trying to coerce God and would be foolish and useless, as well as irreverent.

You do not have to compel God to give you good things, any more than you have to use your will power to make the sun rise. You do not have to use your will power to conquer an unfriendly deity or to make stubborn and rebellious forces do your bidding.

The thinking substance is friendly to you and is more anxious to give you what you want than you are to get it.

To get rich, you need only to use your will power upon yourself.

When you know what to think and do, you must use your will to compel yourself to think and do the right things. That is the legitimate use of the will in getting what you want—to use it in holding yourself to the right course. Use your will to keep yourself thinking and acting in the certain way.

Do not try to project your will or your thoughts or your mind out into space to act on things or people. Keep your mind at home. It can accomplish more there than elsewhere.

Use your mind to form a mental image of what you want and to hold that vision with faith and purpose. Use your will to keep your mind working the right way.

The more steady and continuous your faith and purpose, the more rapidly you will get rich because you will make only positive impressions upon formless substance. You will not neutralize or offset them by negative impressions.

The formless substance receives a picture of your desires and allows this picture to penetrate it to great distances—perhaps, throughout the entire universe.

As this impression spreads, all things are set moving toward its realization. Every living thing, every inanimate thing, and the things yet uncreated are stirred toward bringing into being that which you want. All force begins to be exerted in that direction. All things begin to move toward you. The minds of people everywhere are influenced toward doing the things necessary to fulfilling your desires. And, they work for you unconsciously.

But you can check all this by starting a negative impression in the formless substance. Doubt or unbelief is as certain to start a movement away from you as faith and purpose are to start one toward you. By not understanding this, most people fail when they try to make use of 'mental science' to get rich. Every hour and moment you spend in giving heed to doubts and fears, every hour you spend in worry, every hour in which your soul is possessed by unbelief—sets a current away from you through the whole domain of the intelligent substance. "All the promises are unto them that believe, and unto them only." Notice how insistent Jesus was upon this point of belief. Now you know the reason why.

Since belief is all important, it behooves you to guard your thoughts. And, as your beliefs will be shaped to a very great extent by the things you observe and think about, it is important that you focus your attention. Here the will comes into use, because by means of your will, you determine the objects of your attention.

If you want to become rich, you must not make a study of poverty. Things are not brought into being by thinking about their opposites. Health is never to be attained by studying disease and thinking about disease. Righteousness is not to be promoted by studying sin and thinking about sin. And, no one ever got rich by studying poverty and thinking about poverty.

Medicine as a science of disease has increased disease. Religion as a science of sin has promoted sin. And, economics as a study of poverty will fill the world with wretchedness and want.

Do not talk about poverty. Do not investigate it or concern yourself with it. Never mind what its causes are. You have nothing to do with them. What concerns you is the cure.

Do not spend your time in charitable work or charity movements. All charity only tends to perpetuate the wretchedness it aims to eradicate.

I do not say that you should be hard-hearted or unkind and refuse to hear the cry of need. But, you must not try to eradicate poverty in any of the conventional ways. Put poverty behind you, put all that pertains to it behind you, and 'make good.'

You cannot hold the mental image which is necessary to make you rich if you fill your mind with pictures of poverty. Do not read books or papers which give accounts of the wretchedness of the tenement dwellers or of the horrors of child labor. Do not read anything which fills your mind with gloomy images of want and suffering. You cannot help the poor in the least by knowing about these things. The widespread knowledge of the circumstances of the poor does not tend at all to do away with poverty.

What tends to do away with poverty is not the getting of pictures of poverty into your mind, but getting pictures of wealth into the minds of the poor.

You are not deserting the poor in their misery when you refuse to allow your mind to be filled with pictures of that misery.

Poverty can be done away with, not by increasing the number of well-to-do people who think about poverty, but by increasing the number of poor people who succeed in getting rich through the exercise of faith and purpose.

The poor do not need charity. They need inspiration. Charity only sends them a loaf of bread to keep them alive in their wretchedness or gives them an entertainment to make them forget for an hour or two. But, inspiration will cause them to rise out of their misery. If you want to help the poor, demonstrate to them that they can become rich; prove it by getting rich yourself. Get rich. This is the best way that you can help the poor.

The only way in which poverty will ever be banished from this world is by getting a large and constantly increasing number of people to practice the teachings of this book.

People must be taught to become rich by creation, not by competition.

Every person who becomes rich by competition kicks down the ladder by which he rises and keeps others down. But, every person who gets rich by creation opens a way for thousands to follow him and inspires them to do so.

You are not showing hardness of heart or an unfeeling disposition when you refuse to pity poverty or to think or talk about it or to listen to those who do talk about it. Use your will power to keep your mind off the subject of poverty and to keep your mind fixed with faith and purpose on the vision of what you want.

10

Further Use of the Will

You cannot retain a true and clear vision of wealth if you are constantly turning your attention to opposing pictures, either external or imaginary.

Do not tell others of any past financial troubles. Do not think of them at all. Do not tell anyone about the poverty of your parents or the hardships of your early life. To do any of these things is to mentally class yourself with the poor for the time being, and this will certainly check the movement of things in your direction.

"Let the dead bury their dead," as Jesus said.

Put poverty and all things that pertain to poverty completely behind you.

You have accepted a certain theory of the universe as being correct and are resting all your hopes of happiness on its being correct. What can you gain by giving heed to conflicting theories?

Do not read religious books which tell you that the world is soon coming to an end. Do not read the writings of muckrakers and pessimistic philosophers who tell you that it is going to the devil. The world is not going to the devil. It is going to God. It is a wonderful becoming.

True, there may be a good many things in existing conditions which are disagreeable. But, what is the use of studying them when they are certainly passing away and when the study of them only tends to check their passing and keep them with us? Why give time and attention to things which are being removed by evolutionary growth, when you can hasten their removal only by promoting the evolutionary growth as far as your part of it goes?

No matter how horrible the apparent conditions may be in certain countries, sections, or places, you waste your time and destroy your own chances by considering them. You should interest yourself in the world's becoming rich.

Think of the riches the world is coming into, instead of the poverty it is growing out of. And, bear in mind that the only way in which you can assist the world in growing rich is by growing rich yourself through the creative method—not the competitive one.

Give your attention wholly to riches; ignore poverty. Whenever you think or speak of those who are poor, think and speak of them as those who are becoming rich—as those who are to be congratulated rather than pitied. Then they and others will catch the inspiration and begin to search for the way out.

Because I say that you are to give your whole time and mind and thought to riches, it does not follow that you are to be sordid or mean.

To become really rich is the noblest aim you can have in life because it includes everything else.

On the competitive plane, the struggle to get

rich is a godless scramble for power over other people, but when we come into the creative mind, all this is changed.

All that is possible in the way of greatness and soul unfoldment—of service and lofty endeavor—comes by way of getting rich. All is made possible by the use of things.

If you do not have physical health, you will find that its attainment is conditional on your getting rich. Only those who are emancipated from financial worry and who have the means to live a carefree existence and follow hygienic practices can have and retain health.

Moral and spiritual greatness is only possible for those who are above the competitive battle for existence. And, only those who are becoming rich on the plane of creative thought are free from the degrading influences of competition. If your heart is set on domestic happiness, remember that love flourishes best where there is refinement, a high level of thought, and freedom from corrupting influences. These are to be found only where riches are attained without strife or rivalry by the exercise of creative thought.

I repeat: you can aim at nothing so great or noble as to become rich. You must fix your attention upon your mental picture of riches—to the exclusion of all that may tend to dim or obscure your vision.

You must learn to see the underlying truth in all things. You must see beneath all seemingly wrong conditions the great one life ever moving forward toward fuller expression and more complete happiness.

It is the truth that there is no such thing as poverty. There is only wealth.

Some people remain in poverty because they are ignorant of the fact that there is wealth for them. These people can best be taught by showing them the way to affluence in your own person and practice.

Others are poor because, while they feel that there is a way out, they are too intellectually indolent to put forth the mental effort necessary to find that way and travel it. And, for these people, the very best thing you can do is to arouse their desire by showing them the happiness that comes from being rightly rich.

Others are poor because, while they have some notion of science, they have become so swamped and lost in a maze of metaphysical and occult theories that they do not know which road to take. They try a mixture of many systems and fail in all. For these, again, the very best thing to do is to show them the right way in your own person and practice. An ounce of doing things is worth a pound of theorizing.

The very best thing you can do for the whole world is to make the most of yourself.

You can serve God and your fellow humans in no more effective way than by getting rich. That is, if you get rich by the creative method and not by the competitive one.

Another thing. I assert that this book gives in detail the principles of the science of getting rich. You do not need to read any other book upon the subject. This may sound narrow and egotistical. However, there is no more scientific method of computation in mathematics than by addition, subtraction, multiplication, and division. No other method is possible. There can be only one shortest distance between two points.

There is only one way to think scientifically, and that is to think in the way that leads by the most direct and simple route to the goal. No person has yet formulated a briefer or less complex system than the one I am describing here. It has been stripped of all nonessentials. When you begin this method, lay all others aside. Put them out of your mind altogether.

Read this book every day. Keep it with you. Commit it to memory. Do not think about other systems and theories. If you do, you will begin to have doubts and to become uncertain and wavering in your thought. Then you will bring negative thought to the formless substance.

After you have made good and become rich, you may study other systems as much as you please. But, until you are quite sure that you have gained what you want, do not read anything else on this subject except the authors mentioned in the preface.

Only read the most optimistic comments on the world's news, just those that are in harmony with your picture.

Also, postpone your investigations into the occult. Do not dabble in theosophy, spiritualism, or kindred studies. It is very likely that the dead still live and are near. But, if they are, let them alone. Mind your own business.

Wherever the spirits of the dead may be, they have their own work to do and their own problems to solve. We have no right to interfere with them. We cannot help them. It is very doubtful whether they can help us or whether we have any right to trespass upon their time if they can. Let the dead and the hereafter alone. Solve your own problem; get rich. If you begin to mix with the occult, you will start mental crosscurrents which will surely bring your hopes to shipwreck. Lastly, this and the preceding chapters have brought us to the following statement of basic facts:

There is a thinking stuff from which all things are made, and which in its original state permeates penetrates, and fills the interspaces of the universe.

A thought in this substance produces the thing that is imaged by the thought.

A person can form things in his thought, and by impressing his thought upon formless substance, can cause the thing he thinks about to be created.

In order to do this, a person must pass from

the competitive to the creative mind. He must form a clear mental picture of the things he wants. And, he must hold this picture in his thoughts with the fixed purpose to get what he wants, and the unwavering faith that he will get what he wants—closing his mind against all that may tend to shake his purpose, dim his vision, or quench his faith.

And, in addition to all this, we shall now see that he must live and act in the certain way.

11

Acting in the
Certain Way

Thought is the impelling force which causes the creative power to act. Thinking in the certain way will bring riches to you, but you must not rely upon thought alone, paying no attention to personal action. That is the rock upon which many otherwise scientific metaphysical thinkers meet shipwreck—the failure to connect thought with personal action.

We have not yet reached the stage of development, in which a person can create directly from the formless substance without nature's processes or the work of human hands. A person must act as well as think.

By thought you can cause the gold in the hearts of the mountains to be impelled toward you. But, it will not mine itself, refine itself, coin itself into double eagles, and come rolling along the roads into your pocket.

Under the impelling force of the Supreme Power, people's affairs will be so ordered that someone will be led to mine the gold for you. And, another person's business transactions will be so directed that the gold will be brought toward you. You must arrange your own business affairs so that you are able to receive it when it comes to you. Your thought makes all things, animate and inanimate, work to bring you what you want.

However, your personal activity must be such that you can rightly receive what you want when it reaches you. You are not to take it as charity or steal it. You must give every person more in use value than he gives you in cash value.

The scientific use of thought consists in forming a clear and distinct mental image of what you want, in holding fast to your purpose to get what you want, and in realizing with grateful faith that you do get what you want.

Do not try to project your thought in any mysterious or occult way with the idea of having it go out and do things for you. That is wasted effort and will weaken your power to think with sanity.

In the preceding chapters, I have fully explained the action of thought in getting rich. You must use your faith and purpose to positively impress your vision upon the formless substance, which has the same desire for more life that you have. And, this vision, received from you, sets all the creative forces at work in and through their regular channels of action, but directed toward you.

It is not your part to guide or supervise the creative process. All you have to do with that is to retain your vision, stick to your purpose, and maintain your faith and gratitude.

But you must act in the certain way so that you can appropriate what is yours when it comes to you—so that you can accept the things in your picture and put them in their proper places.

You can readily see the truth of this. When things reach you, they will be in the hands of other people who will ask an equivalent for them.

You can only get what is yours by giving the other person what is his.

Your pocketbook will not become bottomless; it will not always be full of money without effort on your part.

Receiving is the crucial point in the science of getting rich—right here, where thought and personal action must be combined. There are many people who, consciously or unconsciously, set the creative forces in action by the strength and persistence of their desires. However, they remain poor because they do not provide for the reception of the thing they want when it comes.

By thought, the thing you want is brought to you. By action, you receive it.

Whatever your action is to be, it is evident that you must act now. You cannot act in the past. It is essential to the clearness of your mental vision that you dismiss the past from your mind. You cannot act in the future because the future is not here yet. And, you cannot tell how you will want to act in any future contingency until that contingency has arrived.

Because you are not in the right business or the right environment now, do not think that you must postpone action until you get into the right business or environment. And, do not spend time in the present planning the best course in possible future emergencies. Have faith in your ability to meet any emergency when it arrives.

If you act in the present with your mind on the future, your present action will be with a divided mind and will not be effective. Put your whole mind into present action.

Do not give your creative impulse to the original substance and then sit down and wait for results; if you do, you will never get them. Act now. There is never any time but now, and there never will be any time but now. If you are ever to begin to make ready for the reception of what you want, you must begin now.

Your action must be in your present business or employment and must be upon the persons and things in your present environment.

You cannot act where you are not. You cannot act where you have been, and you cannot act where you are going to be. You can act only where you are.

Do not dwell on whether yesterday's work was well or poorly done. Do today's work well.

Do not try to do tomorrow's work now. There will be plenty of time to do that when tomorrow comes.

Do not try by occult or mystical means to act on people or things that are out of your reach.

Do not wait for a change of environment before you act. Cause a change of environment through action.

You can act upon your present environment so as to cause yourself to be transferred to a better environment.

Hold with faith and purpose the vision of yourself in the better environment, but act upon your present environment with all your heart and with all your strength and with all your mind.

Do not spend any time in day dreaming or castle building. Hold to the one vision of what you want, and act now.

Do not cast about seeking some new thing to do or some strange, unusual, or remarkable action to perform as a first step toward getting rich. For some time to come, your actions will probably be the same as those you have been performing. But, now you will perform those actions in the certain way which will surely make you rich.

If you are engaged in some business and feel that it is not the right one for you, do not wait until you get into the right business before you begin to act. Do not feel discouraged or sit down and lament because you are in the wrong place. No person was ever so misplaced that he could not find the right place, and no person was ever so involved in the wrong business that he could not get into the right business.

Hold the vision of yourself in the right business—with the purpose to get into it and the faith that you will get into it. But, act in your present business. Use your present business as the means of getting a better one, and use your present environment as the means of getting into a better one. Your vision of the right business, if held with faith and purpose, will cause the Supreme Power to move the right business toward you. And, your action—if performed in the certain way—will cause you to move toward the business.

If you are an employee and feel that you must change places in order to get what you want, do not project your thought into space and rely upon it to get you another job. It will probably fail to do so. Hold the vision of yourself in the job you want, while you act with faith and purpose on the job you have, and you will certainly get the job you want.

Your vision and faith will set the creative force in motion to bring it toward you. And, your action will cause the forces in your own environment to move you toward the place you want. In closing this chapter, I will add another statement to our syllabus:

There is a thinking stuff from which all things are made, and which, in its original state, permeates, penetrates, and fills the interspaces of the universe.

A thought in this substance produces the thing that is imaged by the thought.

A person can form things in his thought, and by impressing his thoughts upon formless substance, can cause the thing he thinks about to be created.

In order to do this, a person must pass from

the competitive to the creative mind. He must form a clear mental picture of the things he wants. And, he must hold this picture in his thoughts with the fixed purpose to get what he wants, and the unwavering faith that he will get what he wants—closing his mind to all that may tend to shake his purpose, dim his vision, or quench his faith.

That he may receive what he wants when it comes, a person must act now upon the people and things in his present environment.

12

Efficient Action

You must use your thought as I have directed in the previous chapters. You must begin to do what you can do where you are, and you must do all that you can do where you are.

You can advance only by being larger than your present place. And, no man is larger than his present place who leaves undone any of the work pertaining to that place.

The world is advanced only by those who more than fill their present places.

If no one quite filled his present place, there would be a backslide in everything. Those who do not quite fill their present places are a dead weight upon society, government, commerce, and industry. They must be carried along by others at a great expense. The progress of the world is retarded only by those who do not fill the places they are holding. They belong to a former age and a lower stage or plane of life. Their tendency is toward degeneration. No society could advance if every individual was smaller than his place because social evolution is guided by the law of physical and mental evolution. In the animal world, evolution is caused by an excess of life.

When an organism has more life than can be expressed in the functions of its own plane, it develops the organs of a higher plane, and a new species is originated.

There would never have been new species had there not been organisms which more than filled their places. The law is exactly the same for you. Your getting rich depends upon your applying this principle to your own affairs.

Every day is either a successful day or a day of failure. And, it is the successful days which get you what you want. If every day is a failure, you can never get rich; if every day is a success, you cannot help but get rich.

If there is something that may be done today and you do not do it, you have failed insofar as that thing is concerned. And, the consequences may be more disastrous than you imagine.

You cannot foresee the results of even the most trivial act. You do not know the workings of all the forces that have been set moving in your behalf. Much may be depending on your doing some simple act; it may be the very thing which is to open the door of opportunity to great possibilities. You can never know all the combinations which Supreme Power is making for you in the world of things and of human affairs. Your neglect or failure to do some small thing may cause a long delay in getting you what you want.

Do, every day, all that can be done that day.

There is, however, a limitation or qualification that you must take into account. You are not to overwork or to rush blindly into your business in the effort to do the greatest possible number of things in the shortest possible time.

You are not to try to do tomorrow's work today or to do a week's work in a day.

It is really not the number of things you do, but the efficiency of each separate action that counts.

Every act is, in itself, either efficient or inefficient. Every inefficient act is a failure, and if you spend your life doing inefficient acts, your whole life will be a failure. The more things you do, the worse for you, if all your acts are inefficient ones.

On the other hand, every efficient act is a success in itself, and if every act of your life is an efficient one, your whole life must be a success.

The cause of failure is doing too many things in an inefficient manner and not doing enough things in an efficient manner.

You will see that it is a self-evident proposition that if you do not do any inefficient acts and if you do a sufficient number of efficient acts, you will become rich. If it is possible for you to make each act an efficient one, you see again that the getting of riches is reduced to an exact science, like mathematics.

The matter turns, then, on the question of whether you can make each separate act a success in itself. And, this you can certainly do.

You can make each act a success, because the Infinite is working with you, and the Infinite cannot fail.

The Supreme Power is at your service. To make each act efficient you have only to put your own power into it.

Every action is either strong or weak. When every one is strong, you are acting in the certain way which will make you rich.

Every act can be made strong and efficient by holding your vision while you are doing it and by putting the whole power of your faith and purpose into it.

It is at this point that the people who separate mental power from personal action fail. They use the power of mind in one place and at one time, and they act in another place and at another time. Thus, their acts are not successful in themselves; too many of them are inefficient. But, if you put the Supreme Power in every act, no matter how commonplace, every act will be a success in itself. Every success opens the way to other successes. Your progress toward what you want, and the movement of what you want toward you will become increasingly rapid.

Remember that successful action is cumulative in its results. When a man begins to move toward a larger life, more things attach themselves to him, and the influence of his desire is multiplied. This is because the desire for life is inherent in all things.

Do, every day, all that you can do that day, and do each act in an efficient manner.

In saying that you must hold your vision while you are doing each act—however trivial or commonplace—I do not mean to say that it is necessary at all times to see the vision distinctly to its smallest details. During your leisure hours, you should focus your imagination on the details of your vision in order to fix it firmly in your memory.

If you wish speedy results, spend practically all your spare time in this practice. By continuous contemplation you will get the picture of what you want firmly fixed upon your mind and completely transferred to the mind of the formless substance. Then, in your working hours, you need only to mentally refer to the picture to stimulate your faith and purpose and to put forth your best effort. Contemplate your picture in your leisure hours until your consciousness is so full of it that you can grasp it instantly. You will become so enthusiastic about its bright promises that the mere thought of it will call forth the strongest energies of your whole being.

Let us again repeat our syllabus, and by slightly changing the closing statements, bring it to the point we have now reached.

There is a thinking stuff from which all things are made, and which, in its original state, permeates, penetrates, and fills the interspaces of the universe.

A thought in this substance produces the thing that is imaged by the thought.

A person can form things in his thought, and by impressing his thought upon formless substance, can cause the thing he thinks about to be created.

In order to do this, a person must pass from the competitive to the creative mind. He must form a clear mental picture of the things he wants. And, he must do with faith and purpose all that can be done each day—doing each separate thing in an efficient manner.

13

Getting Into the Right Business

Success, in any particular business, depends for one thing upon your possessing in a well-developed state the faculties required in that business.

Without good musical faculty no one can succeed as a teacher of music. Without exceptional mechanical abilities no one can achieve great success in any of the mechanical trades. Without tact and a flair for commerce no one can succeed in the mercantile pursuits. But, to possess in a well-developed state the faculties required in your particular vocation does not ensure getting rich. There are musicians who have remarkable talent, and who yet remain poor. There are blacksmiths and carpenters who have excellent mechanical ability, but who do not get rich. And, there are merchants with good skills for dealing with people who nevertheless fail.

The different faculties are tools. It is essential to have good tools, but it is also essential that the tools should be used in the right way. One man can take a sharp saw, a square, and a good plane and build a handsome article of furniture. Another man can take the same tools and set to work to duplicate the article, but his production will be a botch. He does not know how to use good tools in a successful way.

The various faculties of your mind are the tools with which you must do the work which is to make you rich. It will be easier for you to succeed if you get into a business for which you are well-equipped with mental tools.

Generally speaking, you will do best in that business which will use your strongest faculties— the one for which you are naturally 'best fitted.' But there are also limitations to this statement. No one should regard his vocation as being irrevocably fixed by the skills with which he was born.

You can get rich in any business because if you have not the right talent for it, you can develop that talent. It merely means that you will have to make your tools as you go along, instead of confining yourself to the use of those with which you were born. It will be easier for you to succeed in a vocation for which you already have the talents in a well developed state. But, you can succeed in any vocation because you can develop any rudimentary talent, and there is no talent of which you have not at least a small amount.

You will get rich most easily if you do that for which you are best fitted. But, you will get rich most satisfactorily if you do that which you want to do.

Doing what you want to do is life. And, there is no real satisfaction in living if we are compelled to do something which we do not like to do and fail to do what we want to do. And, it is certain that you can do what you want to do; your desire to do it is proof that you have within you the power which can do it.

Desire is a manifestation of power.

The desire to play music is a power seeking expression and development. The desire to invent mechanical devices is also a power seeking expression and development.

Where there is no power—either developed or undeveloped—to do a thing, there is never any desire to do that thing. Where there is a strong desire to do a thing, it is proof that the power to do it is strong and only needs to be developed and applied in the right way.

All things being equal, it is best to select a business for which you have the best developed talent. But, if you have a strong desire to engage in any particular line of work, you should select that work as the ultimate goal.

Because you can do what you want to do, it is your right and privilege to follow the business or avocation which will be most congenial and pleasant.

You are not obliged to do what you do not like to do and should not do it except as a means to bring you to your desired work.

If there are past mistakes whose consequences have placed you in an undesirable business or environment, you may be obliged for some time to do what you do not like to do. But, you can make the doing of it pleasant by knowing that it is making it possible for you to come to your desired work.

If you feel that you are not in the right vocation, do not act too hastily in trying to get into another one. The best way, generally, to change a business or an environment is by growth.

Do not be afraid to make a sudden and radical change if the opportunity is presented and if you feel, after careful consideration, that it is the right opportunity. But, never take sudden or radical action when you are in doubt as to the wisdom of doing so.

There is never any hurry on the creative plane. And there is no lack of opportunity.

When you get out of the competitive mind, you will understand that you never need to act hastily. No one else is going to beat you to the thing you want to do. There is enough for all. If one place is taken, another and a better one will be opened for you a little farther on. There is plenty of time. When you are in doubt, wait. Fall back on the contemplation of your vision and increase your faith and purpose. And, by all means, in times of doubt and indecision, cultivate gratitude.

A day or two spent in contemplating the vision of what you want and in earnest thanksgiving that you are getting it, will bring your mind into such close relationship with the Infinite that you will make no mistake when you do act.

There is a mind which knows all there is to know. And, if you have deep gratitude, you can come into close unity with this mind by faith and the purpose to advance in life.

Mistakes come from acting hastily or from

acting in fear or doubt or in forgetfulness of the right motive—which is more life to all and less to none.

As you go on in the certain way, opportunities will come to you in increasing numbers. You will need to be very steady in your faith and purpose and to keep in close touch with the Supreme Power through reverent gratitude.

Do all that you can do in a perfect manner every day, but do it without haste, worry, or fear. Go as fast as you can, but never hurry.

Remember that in the moment you begin to hurry you cease to be a creator and become a competitor. You drop back into the old plane again.

Whenever you find yourself hurrying, stop. Fix your attention on the mental image of the thing you want and begin to give thanks that you are getting it. This exercise of gratitude will never fail to strengthen your faith and renew your purpose.

14

The Impression of Increase

Whether you change your vocation or not, you must direct your present actions to the business in which you are presently engaged.

You can get into the business you want by making constructive use of the business you are already established in—by doing your daily work in the certain way.

And, in so far as your business consists in dealing with other people—whether directly, by telephone, or by letter—the key thought of all your efforts must be to convey to their minds the impression of increase.

Increase is what all men and all women are seeking. It is the urge of the formless intelligence within them to find fuller expression.

The desire for increase is inherent in all nature. It is the fundamental impulse of the universe. All human activities are based on the desire for increase. People are seeking more food, more clothes, better shelter, more luxury, more beauty, more knowledge, more pleasure—more life.

Every living thing is under that necessity for continuous advancement. Where increase of life ceases, dissolution and death set in at once.

People instinctively know this, and hence they are forever seeking more. This law of perpetual increase is set forth by Jesus in the parable of the talents. Only those who gain more retain any. "From him who hath not shall be taken away even that which he hath."

The normal desire for increased wealth is not an evil or a reprehensible thing. It is simply the desire for a more abundant life. And, because it is the deepest instinct of their natures, all men and women are attracted to an individual who can give them more of the means of life.

In following the certain way—as described in the foregoing pages—you are getting continuous increase for yourself, and you are giving it to all with whom you deal. You are a creative center from which increase is given off to all.

Be sure of this, and convey assurance of this fact to every man, woman, and child with whom you come in contact. No matter how small the transaction—even if it is only selling of a stick of candy to a little child—put into this action the thought of increase and make sure that the customer is impressed with the thought.

Convey the impression of advancement with everything you do, so that all people shall receive the impression that you are an advancing man and that you advance all who deal with you. Also, give people who you meet socially the thought of increase.

You can convey this impression by holding the unshakable faith that you are in the way of increase and by letting this faith inspire, fill, and permeate every action. Do everything that you do in the firm conviction that you are an advancing personality, and that you are giving advancement to everybody. Feel that you are getting rich, and that in so doing you are making others rich—that you are conferring benefits on all.

Do not boast or brag of your success or talk about it unnecessarily. True faith is never boastful.

Wherever you find a boastful person, you find one who is secretly doubtful and afraid. Simply feel the faith and let it work out in every transaction. Let every act and tone and look express the quiet assurance that you are getting rich—that you are already rich. Words will not be necessary to communicate this feeling to others. They will feel the sense of increase when they are in your presence, and will be attracted to you.

You must so impress others that they will feel that in associating with you they will get increase for themselves. See that you give them a use value greater than the cash value you are taking from them.

If you always take an honest pride in doing this and let everybody know it, you will always have customers. People will go where they are given increase; and the Supreme Power—which desires increase in everything and which knows everything—will move toward you men and women who have never heard of you. Your business will increase rapidly, and you will be surprised at the unexpected benefits which will come to you. You will be able to make larger combinations, to secure greater advantages, and to go on into a more congenial vocation if you desire to do so.

However, in doing all this, you must never lose sight of your vision of what you want or of your faith and purpose.

Let me here give you another word of caution in regard to motives: beware of the insidious temptation to seek power over other people.

Nothing is so pleasant to the unformed or partially developed mind as the exercise of power or domination over others. The desire to rule for selfish gratification has been the curse of the world. For countless ages, kings and lords have drenched the earth with blood in their battles to extend their dominions. They have not been engaged in an effort to seek more life for all, but to get more power for themselves.

Today, the main motive in the business and industrial world is the same. People marshal their armies of dollars and lay waste the lives and hearts of millions in the same mad scramble for power over others. Commercial kings, like political kings, are inspired by the lust for power.

Jesus saw in this desire for mastery the moving impulse of that evil world he sought to overthrow. Read Matthew 23 and see how he pictures the lust of the Pharisees to be called "master," to sit in the high places, to domineer over others, and to lay burdens on the backs of the less fortunate. Note how he compares this lust for dominion to the brotherly seeking for the common good to which he calls his disciples.

Look out for the temptation to seek authority, to become a master, to be considered as one who is above the common herd, and to impress others by lavish display.

The mind that seeks for mastery over others is the competitive mind, and the competitive mind is not the creative one. In order to master your environment and your destiny, it is not at all necessary that you should rule over your fellows. And, indeed, when you fall into the world's struggle for high places, you begin to be conquered by fate and environment and getting rich becomes a matter of chance and speculation.

Beware of the competitive mind! No better statement of the principle of creative action can be formulated than the favorite declaration of the late Golden Rule Jones: "What I want for myself, I want for everybody."

15

The Advancing Man

W hat I have said in the last chapter applies to the professional and the wage earner as well as to a person who is engaged in mercantile business.

No matter what your profession, if you can give increase of life to others and make them sensible of this gift, they will be attracted to you, and you will get rich. The physician who holds the vision of himself as a great and successful healer—and who works toward the complete realization of that vision with faith and purpose—will come into such close touch with the Infinite that he will be phenomenally successful. Patients will come to him in throngs.

No one has a greater opportunity to carry into effect the teachings of this book than the practitioner of medicine. It does not matter which of the various schools he may belong to, because the principle of healing is common to all of them and may be reached by all. The advancing man in medicine—who holds to a clear mental image of himself as successful and who obeys the laws of faith, purpose, and gratitude—will cure every curable case he undertakes, no matter what remedies he may use.

In the field of religion, the world cries out for clergy who can teach their hearers the true science of abundant life. A person who masters

the details of the science of getting rich—
together with the allied sciences of being well,
of being great, and of winning love—and who
teaches these details from the pulpit, will never
lack for a congregation. This is the gospel that
the world needs. It will give increase of life.
People will hear it gladly and will give liberal
support to the person who brings it to them.

What is now needed is a demonstration of the
science of life from the pulpit. We want
preachers who can not only tell us how, but who
in their own persons will show us how. We need
the preacher who is rich, healthy, great, and
beloved, to teach us how to attain these things.
And, when that person comes, he will find a
numerous and loyal following.

The same is true of the teacher who can inspire
the children with the faith and purpose of the
advancing life. That person will never be out of a
job. And teachers who have this faith and purpose
can give it to their pupils. They cannot help giving
it to them if it is part of their own life and
practice.

What is true of the teacher, preacher, and
physician is also true of the lawyer, dentist, real
estate person, insurance agent—of everybody.

The combined mental and personal action I
have described is infallible. It cannot fail. Every
man and woman who follows these instructions
steadily, perseveringly, and to the letter will get
rich. The law of the increase of life is as
mathematically certain in its operation as the law

of gravitation. Getting rich is an exact science.

The wage earner will also find this to be true. Do not feel that you have no chance to get rich because you are working where there is no visible opportunity for advancement—where wages are small and the cost of living high. Form your clear mental vision of what you want and begin to act with faith and purpose.

Do all the work you can do, every day, and do each piece of work in a perfectly successful manner. Put the power of success and the purpose of getting rich into everything that you do. However, do not do this merely with the idea of currying favor with your employer in the hope that he, or those above you, will see your good work and advance you. It is unlikely that they will do so.

The person who is merely a good worker— filling his place to the very best of his ability and satisfied with that—is valuable to his employer. It is not in the employer's interest to promote him. He is worth more where he is.

To secure advancement, something more is necessary than to be too large for your place. The person who is certain to advance is the one who is too big for his place and who has a clear concept of what he wants to be—who knows that he can become what he wants to be and who is determined to be what he wants to be.

Do not try to more than fill your present place with a view to pleasing your employer. Do it with the idea of advancing yourself. Hold the faith and purpose of increase during work hours, after work hours, and before work hours. Hold it in such a way that every person who comes in contact with you—whether foreman, fellow worker, or social acquaintance—will feel the power of purpose radiating from you. Hold the faith and purpose so that everyone will get the sense of advancement and increase from you. People will be attracted to you, and if there is no possibility for advancement in your present job, you will very soon see an opportunity to take another job.

There is a power which never fails to present opportunity to the advancing man who is moving in obedience to law.

God cannot help helping you if you act in the certain way. He must do so in order to help himself.

There is nothing in your circumstances or in the industrial situation that can keep you down. If you cannot get rich working for a conglomerate, you can get rich on a ten-acre farm. And, if you begin to move in the certain way, you will certainly escape from the clutches of the conglomerates and get on to the farm or wherever else you wish to be.

If a few thousand of its employees would enter upon the certain way, a company would soon be in a bad plight. It would have to give its workers more opportunity or go out of business. Nobody has to work for inadequate pay. The company can keep people in so-called hopeless conditions only so long as there are those who are too ignorant to know of the science of getting rich—or too intellectually slothful to practice it.

Begin this way of thinking and acting, and your faith and purpose will allow you to quickly see any opportunity to better your condition.

Such opportunities will speedily come because the Supreme Power, working in everything and working for you, will bring opportunities to you.

Do not wait for an opportunity to be all that you want to be. When an opportunity to be more than you are now is presented and you feel impelled toward it, take it. It will be the first step toward a still greater opportunity.

There is no such thing possible in this universe as a lack of opportunities for a person who is living the advancing life.

It is inherent in the constitution of the cosmos that all things shall be for the advancing man and work together for his good. And, he must certainly get rich if he acts and thinks in the certain way. So let wage earning men and women study this book with great care and enter with confidence upon the course of action I prescribe. It will not fail.

16

Some Cautions and Concluding Observations

Many people will scoff at the idea that there is an exact science of getting rich. Holding the impression that the supply of wealth is limited, they will insist that social and governmental institutions must be changed before a considerable number of people can acquire wealth.

But, this is not true.

It is true that existing governments keep the masses in poverty, but this is because the masses do not think and act in a certain way. If the masses began to move forward according to my suggestions, neither governments nor industrial systems could check them. All systems would have to be modified to accommodate this forward movement.

If the people had the advancing mind and had the faith that they can become rich, nothing could possibly keep them in poverty.

Individuals may enter upon the certain way—at any time and under any government—and make themselves rich. And, when a considerable number of individuals do so under any government, they will cause the system to be modified so as to open the way for others.

The more men who get rich on the competitive plane, the worse for others. The more who get rich on the creative plane, the better for others.

The economic salvation of the masses can only be accomplished by encouraging a large number of people to become rich by practicing the scientific method set down in this book. These people will show others the way and inspire them with a desire for real life—with the faith that it can be attained and with the purpose to attain it.

For the present, however, it is enough to know that neither the government under which you live nor the capitalistic or competitive system of industry can keep you from getting rich. When you enter upon the creative plane of thought, you will rise above all these things and become a citizen of another kingdom.

But, remember that your thought must stay on the creative plane. You are never to regard the supply as limited or to act in a competitive manner.

Whenever you do fall into old ways of thought, correct yourself instantly, because when you are in the competitive mind, you have lost the cooperation of the Supreme Power.

Do not spend any time in planning how you will meet possible emergencies in the future. You should be concerned with doing today's work in a perfectly successful manner—not with emergencies which may arise tomorrow. You can attend to them as they come.

Do not concern yourself with questions of how you will surmount obstacles which may loom upon your business horizon. Ignore these questions unless you can plainly see that your course must be altered today in order to avoid these obstacles.

No matter how tremendous an obstruction may appear at a distance, you will find that if you continue in the certain way, it will disappear as you approach it—or that a way over, through, or around it will appear.

No possible combination of circumstances can defeat a man or woman who is proceeding to get rich along strictly scientific lines. No man or woman who obeys the law can fail to get rich—any more than one can multiply two by two and fail to get four.

Give no anxious thought to possible disasters, obstacles, panics, or unfavorable combinations of circumstances. There is time enough to meet such things when they present themselves before you in the immediate present. You will find that every difficulty carries with it the wherewithal for its overcoming.

Guard your speech. Never speak of yourself, your affairs, or of anything else in a discouraged or discouraging way.

Never admit the possibility of failure or speak in a way that implies failure as a possibility.

Never speak of the times as being hard or of business conditions as being doubtful. Times may be hard and business doubtful for those who are on the competitive plane, but they can never be so for you. You can create what you want, and you are above fear.

When others are having hard times and poor business, you will find your greatest opportunities.

Train yourself to think of and to look upon the world as a something which is becoming—which is growing—and to regard seeming evil as being only that which is undeveloped. Always speak in terms of advancement. To do otherwise is to deny your faith, and to deny your faith is to lose it.

Never allow yourself to feel disappointed. You may expect to have a certain thing at a certain time and not get it at that time. This will seem to be a failure. But, if you hold to your faith, you will find that the failure is only apparent.

Go on in the certain way, and if you do not receive that thing, you will receive something so much better that you will see that the seeming failure was a prelude to a great success.

A student of the science of getting rich had set his mind on making a certain business combination which, at the time, seemed to him to be very desirable. He worked for some weeks to bring it about. When the crucial time came, the thing failed in a perfectly inexplicable way. It was as if some unseen influence had been working secretly against him. He was not disappointed. On the contrary, he thanked God that his desire had been overruled and went steadily on with a grateful mind. In a few weeks, an opportunity so much better came his way that now he would not have made the first deal on any account. He saw that a mind which knew more than he knew had prevented him from losing the greater good by entangling himself with the lesser.

That is the way every seeming failure will work out for you—if you keep your faith, hold to your purpose, have gratitude, and each day, do all that can be done that day.

When you make a failure, it is because you have not asked enough. Keep on, and a larger thing than you were seeking will certainly come to you. Remember this.

You will not fail because you lack the necessary talent to do what you wish to do. If you go on as I have directed, you will develop all the talent that is necessary for doing your work.

It is not within the scope of this book to deal with the science of cultivating talent. But, it is as certain and simple as the process of getting rich.

However, do not hesitate or waver for fear that when you come to a place where you will fail for lack of ability. Keep right on, and when you come to that place, the ability will be furnished to you. The same source of ability, which enabled the untaught Lincoln to do the greatest work in government ever accomplished by a single man, is open to you. You may draw upon the thinking mind to use in meeting the responsibilities which are laid upon you. Proceed in full faith.

Study this book. Make it your constant companion until you have mastered all the ideas contained in it. While you are getting firmly established in this faith, you will do well to give up most recreations and pleasures and to stay away from places where conflicting ideas are advanced in lectures or sermons. Do not read pessimistic or conflicting literature. Spend most of your leisure time in contemplating your vision, in cultivating gratitude, and in reading this book. It contains all you need to know of the science of getting rich. And, you will find all the essentials summed up in the following chapter.

17

A Summary of the Science of Getting Rich

There is a thinking stuff from which all things are made, and which, in its original state, permeates, penetrates, and fills the interspaces of the universe.

A thought in this substance produces the thing that is imaged by the thought.

A person can form things in his thought, and by impressing his thought upon formless substance, can cause the thing he thinks about to be created.

In order to do this, a person must pass from the competitive to the creative mind. Otherwise, he cannot be in harmony with the formless intelligence, which is always creative and never competitive in spirit.

A person can come into full harmony with the formless substance by entertaining a lively and sincere sense of gratitude for the blessings it bestows upon him. Gratitude unifies a person's mind with the thinking mind so that an individual's thoughts are received by the formless substance. A person can remain on the creative plane only by uniting himself with the formless intelligence through a deep and continuous feeling of gratitude.

An individual must form a clear and definite mental image of the things he wishes to have, do, or become. And, he must hold this mental image in his thoughts while being deeply grateful to the Supreme Power for granting him all of his desires. The person who wishes to get rich must spend his leisure hours in contemplating his vision and in earnest thanksgiving that this reality is being given to him. Too much stress cannot be laid on the importance of frequent contemplation of the mental image—coupled with unwavering faith and devout gratitude. This is the process by which the impression is given to the formless substance and the creative forces set in motion.

The creative energy works through the established channels of natural growth and through present industrial and social order. All that is included in his mental image will surely be brought to the person who follows my instructions and whose faith does not waver. What he wants will come to him through the ways of established trade and commerce.

A person must be active in order to receive his own when it is ready to come to him. He must more than fill his present place. He must keep in mind the purpose is to get rich through realization of his mental image. He must do every day all that can be done that day—taking care to do each act in a successful manner. He must give to every man a use value in excess of the cash value he receives—so that each transaction makes for more life. And, he must hold the advancing thought so that the impression of increase will be communicated to all with whom he comes in contact.

The men and women who practice the foregoing instructions will certainly get rich. And, the riches they receive will be in exact proportion to the definiteness of their vision, the fixity of their purpose, the steadiness of their faith and the depth of their gratitude.

Can You Answer these Questions on the Science of Getting Rich?

These questions constitute a thorough examination on this book and a complete outline of the science of financial success. Write out the answer to each question with thoughtful consideration. As far as possible, do so without consulting the book—making sure that you have the principles and practices of the science thoroughly fixed in your memory. Then, reread the chapters and correct your answers. This practice will help you immeasurably in the recognition, realization, and application of this book's principles.

Chapter 1

1. Show that the right to life includes the right to be rich. Tell why in full.
2. Is it right to be content with honest poverty? If not, why not? How rich do you want to be?
3. Explain what a complete life is and show how riches are essential to complete living.
4. In which department of your life—body, mind, or soul—do you feel the greatest lack?

Chapter 2

1. What causes the ownership of money and poverty?
2. Prove that getting rich is not a matter of environment.
3. Prove that getting rich is not the result of superior talent.
4. Prove that getting rich is not the result of saving or thrift.
5. Prove that getting rich is not the result of doing things that are neglected or overlooked by others.
6. Prove that doing things in a certain way is not too difficult to follow.
7. Show how much location is important in getting rich.

Chapter 3

1. Show that opportunity can not be monopolized.
2. Prove that the world's workers have their future in their own hands.
3. What is meant by the "invisible supply?"

Chapter 4

1. How does thought create from the formless substance?
2. What is man, and what power has he?
3. Repeat the summary from page 20/21. Do

you understand it? Do you believe it? How can it be proved?

4.   What is the basic fact behind all appearances?

5.   What must you do and what must you believe if you are to practice the science of getting rich?

Chapter 5

1.   Prove that God wants you to get rich, and tell why.

2.   Why is it essential that your purpose should harmonize with the purpose of the Supreme Power? What is the purpose of the Supreme Power?

3.   Why can you help others more by making the most of yourself than in any other way?

4.   What is the difference between creation and competition?

5.   Explain why God has made plutocrats and monopolists.

6.   Why don't riches gained on the competitive plane cause happiness?

7.   How are you to keep from falling into the competitive mind?

Chapter 6

1.   Explain the difference between use value and market value, and show how one can make a profit without robbing another.

2. If you have wage earners in your employ,
    what can you do to atone for the unfairness
    of the wage system?
3. Can you cause things to be formed directly
    from the atmosphere by thought? How can
    you cause creation? Explain the process.
4. Is it a mistake to ask for a modest
    competence when you can use more?

Chapter 7

1. What are the three steps by which you enter
    into relationship with the Supreme Power?
2. Explain why and how gratitude keeps you
    in close touch with God.
3. Explain the operation of the law of action
    and reaction.
4. Read the four gospels with a special view
    to studying the attitude of Jesus toward the
    Fatherand say what you think of it. How
    does it compare with the attitude suggested
    by this book?
5. Why should you fix your mind on the best?
6. Explain the relation between gratitude and
    faith.
7. Explain why and how all things are good.

Chapter 8

1. What is the most important thing to do to
    make an impression on the thinking
    substance?

2. What is the difference between the dreamer and the person who uses the imagination scientifically?
3. Give your idea as to what constitutes a scientific use of the imagination.
4. Are you working with faith and purpose?

Chapter 9

1. Tell in your own language why you have no right to apply your willpower to other people.
2. Can you compel the things you want to come to you by exerting willpower? If not, why not?
3. Can you keep your mind thinking as you want it to think? If not, what hinders you?
4. Tell how positive and negative impressions are made on the formless substance.
5. What should be your attitude toward poverty?

Chapter 10

1. What about telling others about your past troubles?
2. Explain the use of the will in properly directing the attention.

Chapter 11

1. Why is it impossible to get rich by thought without personal action?
2. What must you do if you are in the wrong business or location?
3. How should an employee proceed to get a better job?

Chapter 12

1. How much should you try to do each day? Why?
2. What is the cause of evolution?
3. How can you make each act efficient?
4. Do you feel that you are acting efficiently now? If not, why not?
5. What is said in this chapter about the vision?

Chapter 13

1. If you have a pronounced talent for some particular business, what should you do?
2. In what way are faculties like tools?
3. What is desire? How does the desire to do a thing prove that you can do the thing?
4. What should you do when tempted to act hastily?

Chapter 14

1. Why do all people desire increase?
2. What assurance should you seek to convey to others?
3. What temptation is spoken of? How much power do you want? Why do you want power?

Chapter 15

1. What impression should the professional person seek to give? Why?
2. What should a worker do who is where there is no visible chance for advancement?
3. What would happen to a company if a few thousand of its employees entered the certain way?

Chapter 16

1. Show why existing governments do not keep the people in poverty.
2. What will accomplish the economic salvation of the masses?
3. What about planning for future emergencies and obstacles?
4. Give the scientific reason for refusing to worry.
5. What are you to do if what you want does not come when you expect it? Give the reason.

6.   What about tasks which look too great for
        your ability?

Chapter 17

1.   Give, in your own words, a summary of the
        science of getting rich.

Additional Programs
and Products
to Help You
Realize Your Potential ...

*"We believe no other speaker alive
teaches these concepts so clearly
and accurately as Bob Proctor."*
Mark Victor Hansen & Jack Canfield,
Co-authors, #1 best-seller,
Chicken Soup for the Soul

The Born Rich Learning System
Are you ready to cash in on the riches inside of you?

BORN RICH gives you the COMPLETE, PROVEN SYSTEM for using the potential you have locked inside of you to achieve financial, emotional, physical and spiritual prosperity.

Recognized worldwide as the most comprehensive personal development learning system available, Bob Proctor's Born Rich System will open your eyes to the deep reservoirs of talent and ability that lie deep inside you. The Born Rich System contains the complete plan for developing the untapped potential in every aspect of your life.

Here's just some of what you will learn in this life-changing program:

- How to successfully balance the spiritual, emotional, intellectual, and physical parts of your being
- Why you are getting the results you are - and how to change any result in your life
- How to use the natural laws of the universe for your maximum benefit
- The most effective way to change any habit
- The little-known secrets of how your mind really works - and how to use them to get the most out of your mental processes
- The Formula for Financial Freedom

What you will receive:

Includes complete 11 1/2 hour workshop on 6 video cassettes presented in 30-45 minute segments for your learning pleasure; 8 audio cassette lessons; international best-selling book, <u>You Were Born Rich</u>; your Personal Action Planner and Goal Card.

The Goal Achiever Success System

The complete system for setting and achieving all of your goals

Regardless of what you would like to achieve, the Goal Achiever Success System will help. The result of a quarter century of research, The Goal Achiever by Bob Proctor contains the COMPLETE SYSTEM for SETTING AND ACHIEVING all of your goals.

You will learn:

- How to bridge the gap between where you are and where you want to be
- The keys to bringing your body, mind and spirit together to effectively realize your dreams.
- The only correct way to decide which goal to work on
- now
  How to work with - instead of against - the natural laws of
- the universe to achieve your goals in the easiest way possible. How to become totally committed to your goal so you will never have to quit and start over again. (No more making
- New Year's resolutions or other goals that you never complete.)
  How to develop a simple Goal Achievement Plan that, when followed daily, will guarantee that you achieve your goal.

When you finish this life-changing program, you will have a thorough understanding of how each element of your being works to bring about the results you are getting in your life. You will know exactly what to do to transform your life into anything that you choose. And, you will have become a Goal Achiever.

What you will receive:
Includes 8 audio cassettes, Goal Card and your Personal Goal Achiever Action Planner

The Winner's Image Success System
Transform yourself into a high-performance winner

Science and psychology have isolated the one prime cause of the results you get in your life: the hidden image you hold of yourself. This self-image operates like the thermostat in your home. Once your image is set, your life is on course to produce the physical manifestation of the mental image you hold.

Bob Proctor's Winner's Image Success System shows you exactly how to set your "personal thermostat" to MAXIMUM SUCCESS so that you can start cruising toward the life of your dreams.

You will learn:

- How to eliminate all competition from your life by moving from the competitive to the creative plane
- The 3 stages of creating your winner's image - and how to move quickly through them
- The Daily 5-Point Program for Materializing Your Winner's Image

What you will receive:

Includes one professionally filmed video cassette, 3 audio cassette lessons and your Personal Action Planner.

"I have shared many hours with Bob Proctor in my home. I am fascinated by his depth of knowledge and understanding of the mind and why we do what we do. Listen to him. He communicates so clearly and effectively. If you want to make a major shift in your life, this man will definitely show you how."
Jay Abraham, Master Marketer,
Fortune 500 Consultant

Mission In Commission Income Acceleration System

How to sell yourself rich and enjoy every minute of it

<u>Bob Proctor used the principles contained in this system to raise himself from a modest salaried position to $1,000,000+ in annual commissions.</u> Using the Mission In Commission system, Bob has taught thousands of salespeople around the globe to do the same.

Here's what you will learn in this powerful program:

- 6 concepts you MUST understand before you will ever earn large commissions
- The one thing you must develop if you want to earn $1,000,000+ in income while still enjoying your work
- The only 3 factors that determine how much money you earn - and why fewer than 1% of the salespeople ever benefit from them
- The PROVEN plan for earning six-figure commissions each and every year.

What you will receive:

Includes 8 professionally-recorded audio cassette lessons, Mission In Commission Card and your personal Mission In Commission Action Planner.

The Science of Getting Rich System
Complete Wealth Creation Program

> *There is a thinking stuff from which all things are made, and which, in its original state, permeates, penetrates, and fills the interspaces of the universe. A thought in this substance produces the thing that is imaged by the thought. A person can form things in his thought, and by impressing his thought upon formless substance, can cause the thing he thinks about to be created.*
>
> —Excerpt from The Science of Getting Rich

Bob Proctor and LIFESUCCESS Productions have created three powerful action tools for turning <u>The Science of Getting Rich</u> into a way of life. This personal growth program is unique. It contains more than information; it is full of WISDOM.

INCOME ACCELERATION GUIDE - The guide has been designed to assist you in taking the wealth creation ideas from <u>The Science of Getting Rich</u> book and implementing them.

AUDIO TAPES - This album of cassettes captures Proctor's dynamic presentation and his deep understanding of <u>The Science of Getting Rich</u>; an understanding which has been developed from years of studying Wallace D. Wattles' masterpiece. Bob Proctor will lead you through your **INCOME ACCELER-ATION GUIDE.**

The **SPECIAL EDITION** *"The Science of Getting Rich"* **BOOK** with Bob Proctor's personal introduction.

The Success Puzzle

Why is Success a Puzzle?

What has been holding you back from living your dreams and getting exactly what you want in your life? Why is success so puzzling?

Each one of you has your own personal dreams and goals—your very own "success puzzle." Now, Bob Proctor helps by giving you the missing pieces to achieving your ideal life. He likens success to a puzzle: in order to successfully piece together a puzzle, you use the picture on the puzzle box lid as a guide. If you don't have a picture of the puzzle to follow, it's difficult to complete. The same is true of success. In order to get what you want out of life, you must have a clearly defined image or goal to work toward. *The Success Puzzle* shows you how to put together the framework to get to where you want to go.

Bob Proctor gives you cutting-edge concepts that will lead you through the Success Guidebook so you can create your own personal success map. You'll discover exactly what you want out of life and how to achieve it.

You will learn:

- How to eliminate obstacles blocking the path to your dreams and goals
- How to create a "success picture" of your life
- How to put the pieces of your life in place to complete your own personal "success puzzle"

MENTORING

Increase Your Income Every Day With
Bob Proctor

- Learn from a Master Mentor on a live one-hour *TeleSEMINAR* every month.

- Receive a Success Study Guide and an exciting written lesson for your monthly *TeleSEMINAR*.

- Receive a book from Bob Proctor's Book of the Month Club every month.

- Enlightening Lessons every week.

- Review your goals quarterly with Bob Proctor

- Listen to Bob Proctor's QuickSTART—A new idea every day.

- A unique cassette library you will be proud to own.

Join Bob Proctor's personal mentoring program and study with him every week. Compound both your income and your effectiveness.

CALL
800-759-4136

Success Series - Volume I and II

More than three decades of study and research has been consolidated into Bob Proctor's Success Series. This remarkable series distills and combines ancient wisdom, the immutable laws of nature and the habits and techniques of modern achievers, into these comprehensive audio programs.

Volume I	Volume II
SUCCESS	ACTION
DECISION	MONEY
RISK	GOALS
PERSISTENCE	ATTITUDE
RESPONSIBILITY	CREATIVITY
CONFIDENCE	COMMUNICATION

Additional Workbooks Available

Share Bob Proctor's life-changing concepts with your friends, family, business associates, sales force or any other group, by ordering additional copies of his Action Planner Workbooks. The following Action Planners are available:

- You Were Born Rich
- The Goal Achiever
- A Winner's Image
- Mission In Commission
- The Success Puzzle

LIFE SUCCESS PRODUCTIONS LEARNING SYSTEM RESERVATION FORM

THREE EASY WAYS TO ORDER:
1. **FAX** this page to **800-317-9679, 24 hrs, 7 days a week**
2. **MAIL** this page to: LifeSuccess Productions, 15651 N. 83rd Way, Suite C3
   Scottsdale, AZ 85260
3. **CALL 800-871-9715**

System Description	Investment	Qty.	Total
Born Rich Learning System	$697	x ___	= _____
The Winner's Image System	$197	x ___	= _____
The Goal Achiever System	$147	x ___	= _____
Mission In Commission System	$147	x ___	= _____
The Success Puzzle System	$139	x ___	= _____
Science of Getting Rich System	$495	x ___	= _____
Success Series - Volume I ❏ or Volume II ❏	$ 99	x ___	= _____
<u>**The Science of Getting Rich**</u> Book	$ 12.^{95}	x ___	= _____
<u>**You Were Born Rich**</u> Book	$ 12.^{95}	x ___	= _____
<u>**Good Grief**</u> Book	$14.^{95}	x ___	= _____
Born Rich Action Planner Workbook	$ 12	x ___	= _____
Goal Achiever Action Planner Workbook	$ 12	x ___	= _____
Winner's Image Action Planner Workbook	$ 12	x ___	= _____
Mission In Commission Action Planner Workbook	$ 12	x ___	= _____

Shipping & Handling $6 per item; $3 per
Born Rich Book or Action Planner;
Max. $20
Please allow 2-3 weeks for delivery
in US; 3-4 weeks in Canada

Prices in US Dollars

SUB TOTAL $ _____

S & H $ _____

TOTAL $ _____

Your Name _____

Address _____

City _____ State/Province _____

Zip/Postal Code _____ Country _____

Phone (H) (___)_____ (W) (___)_____

Fax   (H) (___)_____ (W) (___)_____

Your Profession_____

FINANCING (Check one) ❏ MASTERCARD   ❏ VISA   ❏ AMEX
                   ❏ CHECK (Payable to LifeSuccess Productions)

Credit Card Number_____

Cardholder's Name (as on Card) _____

Exp. Date _____ Signature _____

100% MONEY-BACK PERSONAL GUARANTEE FROM BOB PROCTOR: Follow the plan in the system you invest in for 60 days. If, at the end of that time, you have put the ideas into use and are not thrilled with the results, you may return the products with a note describing what actions you took based on the ideas you learned, and I will personally refund 100% of your investment any time up to 90 days from the date of your purchase. (You must call first to get a return authorization number before returning your products.)